Loss Within Waves

By Elizabeth Johnstone

with NextGen Story: Custom Publishing

Photographs of paintings by Alberto Porro @_albertoporro_

Edited by Daphne Ffoulkes-Jones and David Holmes. Copy-edited by Kerry Davie.

Cover art by Elizabeth Johnstone, design of cover and interior by Kim Lajeunesse.

Published by NextGen Story: Custom Publishing

www.nextgenstory.com

Acknowledgements

I have to start by thanking my family. Daniel and Finn for the joy you bring me daily. My parents, my sister, and my brother for your patience and love. My mother-in-law for your continued kindness and my father-in-law for always driving me to my therapy appointments. My friends and colleagues for meeting me where I was at. Dr. Kattan and Dr. Zargapour for your guidance and listening ear, and for allowing me space to acknowledge what was painful and difficult but not insurmountable. Louna, for your care and support and for the dedication of the obstetrics and gynecology (OBGYN) medical team at the Jewish General Hospital. Norma for reading my first writings. Mali and the NextGen Story Custom Publishing team for helping me to navigate this exciting journey towards publishing.

Table of Contents

Preface

This work did not start as a book. It was a collection of journal writings and reflections on my experience with grief. Seven years later, I had a treasure trove of my inner thoughts and experiences centered on the most traumatic time of my life along with its aftermath and residual effects. People had told me that the early blog writings that I had shared had helped them through something similar. I toyed with the idea of sharing my writing through publication and had a close friend and colleague read my writings. Her heartfelt feedback gave me the encouragement to move forward and to team up with Mali from NextGen Publishing. This led to edits but also to new emerging thoughts and even paintings that were produced in response to reflections on my writings. Here I am now, vulnerably opening my writing to others, hoping that my experience will offer some support to them. Hopefully my book will also give some understanding to those who were close to me and who watched from the outside. For those who wonder what I must have been going through, it may help shed some light. In this book I hope to take you through tidal waves of grief and show it is possible to pass through them without drowning.

While the grief experience may be different for every person, there are common realities voiced by many who go through it.

Sometimes grief is felt as a little wave that passes within a few minutes. At other times, grief feels like a tidal wave, wiping us out completely.

Something heard, remembered, or seen can bring it up unexpectedly. There is no order or reason for grief.

Misplaced feelings of guilt and self judgement can be embedded in the experience.

A grieving person needs accompaniment on the often-lonely journey by someone who expects or anticipates nothing but is simply willing to walk alongside them.

The healing journey encourages being honest and transparent with ourselves and giving ourselves time and space to feel what we are feeling.

How do I see my experience through time thus far? I feel that I can now stand and observe the experiences from before without judging them and brace myself with steady breaths for what is yet to come.

Prologue

Stuck Between Wanting to Remember and Trying to Forget

I wasn't sure that I wanted children until finally I did. Up until then, counselling teenagers and caring for them was both fulfilling and a life calling. I felt that I was impacting individuals at key points in their lives and knew that having a family might take away from that dedicated focus. Daniel and I had been together for nearly twelve years and had been married for four when I began to long for motherhood. Getting pregnant wasn't automatic. I was impatient and a little heartbroken every month when it didn't happen. After eight months of trying, I was discouraged. I wondered if it would ever happen. Then, in 2015 when I was thirty, after a spring break vacation, I found out that I was pregnant—with our baby due at the end of November. We were very excited, but oblivious to what lay ahead for us as new parents.

I began writing down my thoughts in July 2015 to help me process what was happening to us, to me, and to our growing child. But as a warning to you the reader, what I've written and what I've decided to share is at times tragic and is likely triggering for many who have experienced the longing for and loss of a pregnancy or—even worse—the death of a child. I was a very open, transparent individual before this trauma. But it changed and silenced me for a long time. For many years it prevented me from sharing verbally and connecting with others (even those closest to me). It is something I've only recently come to terms with. However, I believe I can now be open about sharing some very deep and personal pain, and the harsh realities of living and surviving with post-traumatic stress disorder (PTSD).

I'd hoped to quickly process the loss of our son and to move on—to serve as an example to others. To be a symbol of hope and resilience and of faithful dedication for those living through one of the worst moments of their lives. I imagined myself a sturdy boat rocked by the waves, but one that remained buoyant and intact regardless of the tempest. I now know that reality is much less picturesque.

Through my experience I've realized that it is more meaningful to share my struggles honestly, and to recognize the sense of shame that I felt for not being able to pull myself out of them on my own. It took me eight years to get to where I am today—to be able to become, at least partly, the person that I was before. It has been a long and unexpected journey. At first while writing personal blog posts, and then while journaling for myself before and after my second pregnancy, I began the process of healing. I sought counselling on two separate occasions, and immersed myself in mindfulness and different artforms, all with the goal of keeping myself from drowning emotionally during this most traumatic of times. All through my grieving, my family stood by me, often having to watch from a distance (as I deliberately kept them at arm's length). I thought that I was protecting them from what was really going on inside me.

These past two years I built up the courage to decide to take my accumulated words and artwork and compile them into a book that I could share. It's now time to let others back into my life. I'm ready. I hope that through the sharing of my journey I will motivate others to courageously seek the support they need, in whatever form it takes. This act of sharing is in essence the final chapter in my healing journey. Thank you for wanting to take this journey with me.

The act of writing this book was an epic trek all on its own. Over many long months I looked over my earlier writings. I reflected, painted, and saw within those paintings insights that had yet to surface. This inspired me to write even more. Art softened what I was feeling and gave it physical substance. Words helped to clear my head and heart of the heaviness they bore. The use of language also helped to make sense of what I was living, thinking, and feeling. Time was also vital, as it provided the necessary space to get me to where I am today.

This book is a journey through the stages and inner reflections of my personal grief. The first stage is about my pregnancy and its accompanying hopeful spirit. The second stage is about the tidal wave of loss and the desperate act of pushing others away. The third stage is about the realization that I could not tread water anymore, and, after being diagnosed with PTSD, all the therapy that followed. The last stage is about living with and loving our second child, while learning how to integrate the sadness that still exists in our lives with the happy and joyful family that we have become.

Prelude

I have realities in my past, not only the reality of work done and of love loved, but of sufferings bravely suffered. These sufferings are even the things of which I am most proud, though these are things which cannot inspire envy.

—Viktor Frankl

Little T is often on my mind. It doesn't take much to remind me of him. There are so many memories that surface throughout the year—memories from the year he grew in my belly, and memories of the years that came after as grief and the PTSD symptoms appeared, threatening to wash away any future happiness. Maybe I spend too much time looking for things to remind me of him. I may still be stuck somewhere between remembering and the impossible task of trying to forget.

In reading Viktor Frankl's book Man's Search for Meaning, I was struck by his reflection on the healing process and how he suggested that, in order to heal, a person must find meaning in the loss.

I feel a great desire to share the story of Little T's life with others, and how his life has inspired such a profound change on my own. It's more than just a record of what he taught me. His story gives his life deep meaning and shows how much of an impact his existence did have, and continues to have, in this world. I don't want his memory to be lost and without purpose. This is why I have decided to share my writings, my personal experiences with grief, and the challenges I have found in living with grief.

Life is taking form

Hope and joy is what we rest on

There is little knowledge or foundation

Knowing, planning what is next is futile

One day at a time

What is next except to keep looking forward

Faith to fall on, to help hold us up

SECTION 1

Expecting and Holding on to Hope

Theodore a.k.a. "Little T" Bartlett

From July to November 2015, I wrote blog posts and crafted occasional emails to inform those in my life what was going on with my thirty-six-week pregnancy with Little T. It began in order to simply provide details—so I didn't have to repeat everything—as the medical information was daunting. However, it soon became a way to express to others what I was going through, what I needed, and more importantly what I didn't need from them.

The audience of the blog posts were people close to me: friends, family members, and colleagues. The occasional email served to inform a closer subset of people who were often my more intimate family. This was the first blog post that I published.

July 26, 2015

Blog Post; **"Introduction to Characters and Situation."**

This blog is open only to those who personally know us; as such, I am not going to make any introductions, except to say that after having been together for over twelve years, and married for the past five, we are now expecting a baby in late November to early December. Oh yeah, and we are very happy together. ;)

If you haven't heard yet, here it is. . . .

I had my first scheduled ultrasound at twenty weeks on July 13, just as I was about to finish work for the summer. Unfortunately, our doctor spotted an abnormality in the baby's heart, but he couldn't tell us more than that. He referred us right away to the cardiology department of St. Justine Hospital, and he told us that they should be able to see us within ten days.

On July 16 we ended up meeting with our new OBGYN in that hospital's high-risk pregnancy clinic. I had another ultrasound, and he did an amniocentesis and took swabs for DNA testing. We also met with a geneticist from the Jewish General who explained what it was that they were testing for. Lastly, we met with a cardiologist from the Montreal Children's Hospital who did a thorough ultrasound of the baby's heart. Unfortunately, the news wasn't good.

Our baby not only has a rare condition, but it also shows signs of a medical condition even rarer than that. One of the baby's heart arteries is too small. It isn't allowing blood to flow to the lungs which then prevents the blood from becoming re-oxygenated. This is called Tetralogy of Fallot. Until birth, this isn't a problem—but afterwards it will be and it will require immediate repair. Another issue (as if that isn't enough) is that there is a missing valve in the pulmonary artery. (Basically, a door which allows the flow of blood in and out is missing.) Lastly, one of the arteries (the one missing the valve) is much bigger than it should be. As a result, the baby's heart is now working too hard, and the fear is that the artery might cause pressure on the lungs and trachea, preventing them from developing normally.

The most frustrating thing is that there is nothing to be done during the pregnancy. The baby needs to go to full term and will then need surgery, hopefully at around three months of age. These conditions will likely require the baby to have more surgeries throughout their life. With the six other cases that the Children's Hospital has dealt with during the last two years, all but one have made it to two years thanks to surgery(s). That infant died at six weeks in the pregnancy due to other complications.

We are presently waiting for the genetic testing results. These will help determine if some genetic disorder has caused this abnormality, and if so, what other things could happen (go wrong) other than with the heart. It will also help determine if this could re-occur in future pregnancies. We are hoping, of course, that this is not due to a genetic condition.

This has all been a huge blow, but we are feeling okay despite everything. Before seeing the cardiologist, we had been hoping for better news. Finding out that we have the rarest form of an already rare condition is very hard to wrap our heads around.

My health is completely fine, though, and I am in no danger whatsoever. Other than the baby's heart problems, the pregnancy is going well, and the baby's development is on track. We will have our follow-up appointment in four weeks with the OBGYN from the Jewish General. At the end of September, the Children's will take over and the baby will be delivered there in November.

It has been good to have some time for the two of us. Daniel has taken some days off in July. When we are together it seems to make it all easier. Our families are very supportive and respect us when we just need time alone. We are feeling much more accepting of the whole thing and realize that there is much we can't control; worrying about it will not have any benefit. We must take it day by day.

Things you can be praying for:

That the baby's enlarged heart will not cause any damage to the development of the lungs or trachea.

That despite the baby's heart needing to work harder, this will not prevent the baby from making it to at least thirty-six weeks.

Strength and courage for us both and for our families.

Thanks again and as always for all your love and support.

Liz and Daniel

July 29, 2015

Blog Post; **"More Unique Than We Would Ever Ask For."**

An update is in order.

We heard back from the geneticist earlier than expected. We met with her today (July 29) and the news wasn't what we wanted to hear. The abnormality shown so far in the baby's development—the heart abnormality—is caused by a chromosome irregularity. Yet again, we are unique. The baby has an abnormality in the twelfth chromosome. Specifically, there has been a duplication of two sections of the twelfth chromosome of one of our sets (the baby gets two sets, one from each of us).

The duplication of the first section has been previously reported in only three other cases worldwide. In these cases, the duplication has caused the child language delays, intellectual deficiencies, developmental delays, and, during the pregnancy itself, developmental delays. What the geneticist was clear on saying was that we could expect to see the same with our baby but to what degree, no one could predict.

The duplication of the second section is the first case ever reported worldwide. That's how rare this is. It means that we have no cases to compare with in order to predict what this could mean for the baby. They don't even know what all the genes in that section are responsible for. They assume, though, that the severe heart abnormality falls under this duplication error. Again, what this might further incur is unknown.

How did this happen? Maybe one of us passed down this chromosome with abnormalities in it or maybe it was a fluke of nature. They will do more genetic tests now on our chromosomes, but this will only answer whether such a thing could occur again with our future children. It won't change anything for this baby in terms of prevention or intervention.

July 30, 2015

Blog Post; **"Letting you in but Keeping you Out."**

I think it's a good time to be open about what we are going through emotionally, as I know many of you are concerned for us.

Firstly, please act normally around us: invite us to things as usual, and talk to us about your lives and what is going on. Don't bring this up unless we do. Please don't say how sorry you are. A better way to express it is: "I am thinking about and praying for you." We don't need to be reminded of what is wrong all the time. We don't want to talk about it, but we are willing to let you in on what we are feeling and going through.

For my own sake, I thought it would be helpful to share the following thoughts and reflections that I have put together, including ones on how best to care for us.

I don't seem to be able to talk about this stuff as much as I thought I would, except with Daniel (who I am very grateful for). I always thought of myself as open, vulnerable, and willing to express whatever I felt—to be more than willing to have people around who could listen and be supportive. Surprisingly, I now find that difficult, or at least I am now very cautious, as I really don't want to hear what others (besides Daniel, really) have to say; I don't want to hear what comforting things they might try to offer in words.

I am fragile now and want to protect myself. I think I am good at knowing what I need; the words of people who are not directly going through what we are going through are not what I need right now. In fact, I find myself getting annoyed or angry at comments made by people, well-meaning or not. The gift of understanding is truly a gift that very few possess. Being able to put yourself in someone else's shoes is very difficult. This is an ability that I really believed that I had. But I never could have imagined that we'd be going through what we have been during the last three weeks. Neither do I have the words or ways to comfort myself in this situation. Therefore, it's better to not presume that you can. Not to be mean about it—but people simply cannot understand what we are feeling and going through. Therefore, I really don't want people to try.

One thing that is not helpful is to hear from people, "You never know, a miracle can happen, and things might be completely fine by the time the baby's born." I have faith. I do believe in miracles. But firstly, why should we be the ones to get a miracle when there are so many others who are suffering in the world and who do not have the kind of access to health care and support that we have? Secondly, I believe that advances in science are a way for God to work miracles. Understanding the human body and how babies develop in the womb is truly miraculous. For medical professionals to now have the ability to carry out tests and then determine what can be done for our little baby at this stage in its development is miraculous and quite new. If you had been with us during our various conversations with medical professionals (when we looked at the ultrasounds and genetic results, etc.), you would understand why it is not helpful to expect us to be able to turn back the clock so that suddenly there were no longer any signs of abnormalities.

Do we pray in solitude for a miracle? Yes. Do we encourage others to privately pray for us? Yes. But telling us that maybe things will turn around just isn't helpful.

What we need now is to emotionally prepare for whatever is to come. It is certain that our baby will need many surgeries. It is a reality that we are special needs parents and that quote unquote "normal parenting" is not in store for us. With that said, would everyone like to change this fact? Of course. But, in order to be the best parents to our child, we need to move past that. We need to prepare emotionally to be ready to love our baby no matter what the challenges are that come with it—of which it is fair to say we can expect many.

It is a great comfort to me to know that people are thinking about us and praying for us and the baby. That is—as long as I am not there when they are doing that. I feel and know how many people care about us. If you think of us, please say continued prayers.

I know some people may be worrying about us. I don't want you to. That is easier said than done, I know, but please know the following:

- We have never been stronger as a couple. We are leaning on each other and being entirely open with each other in what and how we feel and what we are experiencing in all of this. We are kind to each other and we do not take our frustrations or our irritableness out on each other, even though we are more sensitive right now. We take time to be with each other (and with friends and family)—to have fun and to enjoy many things together. Our life has not ended, we still have many things going on and we aren't shying away from people, unless it's because of the things mentioned above.

- We have wonderfully supportive families, which we are grateful for.

- We have not given up on our faith. I will blog about just

this for those who are interested.

- As as long as it continues to be helpful for me, I will continue to communicate what we are going through.

Thanking you in advance for your understanding and for all the love and support.

August 4, 2015

Blog Post; **"Faith Shattered or Strengthened."**

While not everyone reading this may share a religious faith as I do, it might still interest you to know where I am in my faith journey since up to this point it has been a part of my life and it may help you to understand where I am coming from.

I don't think that either of us were ever of a mindframe to blame God for all the bad things in this world and all the heartbreaking things that happen. This seems to have carried over to our personal situations as well. Everything I understand about God, and why I have never walked away from religion/faith, whatever you want to call it, is because I understand God to be a loving God. When religion hasn't demonstrated this, I blame it on our human nature, not God.

I understand God to be one who is present all the time but probably, and most meaningfully, when you need Him most, when you are incapable of handling what is in front of you, and when you are willing to let go and admit that you have no control over things. He is most present in those moments, and both Daniel and I have felt this. Trust me when I say that God has been witness to every one of our thoughts and I think that I am having more inner dialogues with Him now than I have had in a long time. I don't think anyone can judge us for the fact that this dialogue has not exclusively been one of thanksgiving during these past three weeks, but we have found many things to be thankful to Him for. Personally, I could not feel more blessed to have Daniel alongside of me to go through all of this with. The person he is gives me a lot of strength and the courage to be able to face whatever comes.

Have we felt anger? Some, but not too much, partly because we realize the futility of it. What good in the end would it bring to suppose that someone is to blame? What good would it do to throw up our hands and ask God, "Why us? Why do we deserve this?" It's not something we have really entertained. Someone I know who went through a very difficult personal struggle this past year said it best. "Why should anyone else deserve this?" I wouldn't wish this upon anyone, and why are we better or worse than anyone else that we should get more blessings or less personal tragedy/ trauma than someone else?

I think karma is a load of crap and believing in it doesn't do anything to make this world a better place. I think the book of Job is clearly placed in the Bible to show that faith in God is not about doing good actions in order to receive blessings/rewards. This life we lead is full of challenges and heartaches. Faith isn't meant to shelter "believers" from experiencing these. It's meant to equip us for them and to remind us that our actions and our love and kindness can be a way that we offer God's love to each other, and a way to make us brave for this life.

One thing I am very clear about is that God did not wish this pain and heartache on us. If someone approaches me and tells me that this is God's will for us . . . beware, they may get their face ripped off! Why someone would believe this is beyond me, and I feel very badly if this is your view of God.

If you believe in God, this is what I ask—that you pray for us and share with us. God will be with us through this; He will strengthen us and teach us how to be the loving parents that we will have to be in order to face everything that our child will need. Don't think that we need to hear your thoughts about what God is trying to teach us through all of this—honestly you can keep those to yourself. Read the book of Job if you want to get a sense of why those comments are irrelevant and unhelpful.

Our faith hasn't been shattered; if anything, we are realizing more than ever how important it is to believe that a Higher Power is with us every day—a Power that will equip us and teach us how to love more than we could ever manage on our own.

August 24, 2015

Blog Post; **"An Update is in Order."**

How do I update you on how we are doing? Well, it probably seems very strange to hear that we are doing quite well, even good I would say. I think it even surprises us. It has been over a month now since the first ultrasound when all the bad news started. I think time has helped us to process things, get over the shock, move away from the raw feelings, and move towards acceptance and, to some extent, normalcy again.

Having fun with friends and family has been a huge help. We have been going to see movies as we usually do, have gone camping for the weekend, and have been doing other things that we love. Very importantly, we have been finding many things to laugh about. Life does in fact continue and these are the things that normally bring us joy. It has been important to keep these things going.

The fun has helped steer me away from worry; it has distracted me if you will. The big worry was that the next ultrasound would bring about more bad news—more signs that the baby's development was also showing delays. Last Tuesday we had our ultrasound appointment, and we were thrilled to learn that this wasn't the case. Our "Little T" (nicknamed Little T-Rex) showed normal all-around growth. He was a good weight, and measurements were normal. The heart, of course, still has serious issues. It must work a lot harder, but it is working and showing no signs of failure. Walking away from that appointment was a huge relief and it gave a feeling of joy. I felt dread start to leave me, and we finally had a positive thing/experience to celebrate. I have been finding myself getting excited again, like I was before, about preparing for Little T's arrival.

Daniel and I have talked about how we feel, now that we are back to where we were before all this dark news. We didn't and still don't know what to expect in becoming parents. We don't know what to anticipate or how to "prepare." We do know, though, that it will be a big change in our lives, and it will be a welcome one. We might know now that what lies ahead when Little T is born is going to be a huge challenge, one that is much more than we expected and full of uncertainty—but it was before as well.

The baby will be born with a medical team on alert, one ready to help every step of the way, and we are finding comfort in that. I have been thinking about how I would tell my Malawian[1] friends about everything that has been going on with our baby, and I can't help but feel that none of them would even comprehend it. What we already know, even before the birth of the baby, and what surgical options and medical and emotional supports are available to us as Canadians, at no cost, is simply unimaginable for so many others around the world. I have a great sense of gratitude that our baby has options, and that there is hope. We don't need a miracle like others might. Support will be with us all along the way.

---

[1] In 2008 I began a friendship and long-term partnership with Rodrick Banda from Malawi, Africa. We partnered together to create the non-profits Warm Heart Missions (Malawi) and Warm Heart Initiatives (Canada), I travelled to Malawi in 2008, 2011, and 2014.

I am at a point now where I can enjoy the experience of pregnancy and reflect on how there are only three months to go before Baby T is born. I am excited to be showing a big bump now, although I am feeling heavier. All the while, the experience of Little T digging into me (I don't even know what part of me actually) is, well, unpleasant. But my hair has never looked better, and my full appetite is back. I keep needing to change my wardrobe and to find new solutions for sitting comfortably, as Little T lets me know quickly when my posture isn't right. It's a daily adventure, but one I'd never miss.

August 25, 2015

Blog Post; **"Back to Work."**

I have been back at work for just over two weeks now. I didn't know how I would feel about it, but it has proven to be a good decision. I guess I shouldn't be too surprised as I love my job[2] and work with a hugely supportive team. I find daily value in what I do, which is working with and on behalf of students. I work independently a lot of the time as my superiors trust what I do and value my input and opinions. So far since I have been back, work has involved following up on students' results, looking up what students need in order to get their diplomas, and contacting those who have left our school, in the cases where they still need credits. In those cases I need to remind them of when and where to enroll to finish their diplomas.

A big part of being back to work has been meeting with parents and students who are about to enter their last year of high school. I have been working with the vice principals to find the best path academically for each student, the

_____

[2] I work in a high school and my title is counsellor in academic training.

path that will allow them to achieve the goal of obtaining a diploma. When this goal looks especially challenging—almost unattainable—we try to make sure that the course plan is one that the student can realistically face. I am fortunate to work with administrators who can see how one student's journey to get there will be different from another's, and that students having a voice and buy-in is essential.

The students and teachers aren't back yet, but that's just around the corner. When students return, my role also becomes one of providing a haven for students who are often struggling with heavy emotional issues. We offer support through a physical space in the school, but I also meet individually with students as needed, and I coach them on developing healthy coping strategies while getting them to specialized services if required. I don't know yet how I will handle hearing students speak about their personal difficulties, but I would like to try. My work, after all, is all about the students and offering them support and guidance. I will still have a couple of months to do this before Little T is born, and I hope to keep the focus on that while at work.

If working in this capacity has been a validating experience for me in the past, I would think that it will continue to be. Over the past years I have learned the importance of making sure that there is a balance in my life. On the one hand there is work, and on the other hand there is taking time for self-care and the fostering of my relationships and support network. That, of course, is more important now than ever. I can't afford to ignore it. People around me at work will also probably be more cued into recognizing when I am having a hard time and will then push me to stop, step back, and take care of myself first. I take comfort in that. I know that if it becomes too much, I can step back and be at home, but right now, work is where I want to be.

I am not sure how I am going to face students, parents, and staff who will notice my belly and then make comments that pertain to more "normal" pregnancies and life with a newborn. I don't think I will need to worry about the students' comments as much as the adults'. Students aren't going to be offering advice. I don't know if Little T will be able to come home from the hospital right away, or after a time. Maybe what I don't want, if it can be avoided, will be people's stories about what it was like for them when their baby was first born. What advice they will have won't be helpful because our baby's path is very unique. We are okay with that now; we have accepted it. Hearing how different we are from others is still painful, though. Facing things as they come with Little T is what we'll have to do. Hearing comparisons made from others' "normal" experiences won't do us much good.

September 11, 2015

Blog Post; **"Managing Expectations and Parenting."**

An interaction that I had been dreading finally happened today, but to my pleasant surprise it took a sweet turn.

I was walking in the halls today and catching up with a student who I had worked with last year. She has attention deficit hyperactivity disorder (ADHD), and had been getting herself into conflicts by not thinking before she spoke. Suddenly she asked me, "Miss, you don't want to know whether the baby will be a boy or a girl?" I replied, "No, we want to keep it a surprise," to which she responded, "Well it doesn't matter really, as long as the baby is healthy, right?" Being her hyperactive self—so not even looking to register my response—she continued, "And even if it isn't, I know you'll love him or her just the same."

Had she just left the conversation at "as long as the baby is healthy" I would have left the hallway in tears. Instead, without knowing anything about our baby's health concerns— she answered me from her heart and said one of the sweetest things that I have heard from a student.

She continued. "My mom always tells us, 'As long as you are happy.'" With that, she scurried down the hall to class, leaving me taken aback.

"As long as you are happy."

I have been thinking more and more about parenting and managing the expectations that we have before Little T arrives. Not knowing what the future holds for the little trooper as he or she grows is scary and it leaves us often feeling helpless. Health-wise, whether he or she will have learning, physical, or intellectual delays . . . it's all unknown. I suppose that's the case for any parent. No parent can predict what struggles their child will face. One thing I do know is who Daniel and I are to our child; how we treat him or her is the biggest factor in Little T's happiness and it is the only thing that we can really control.

The students that I have worked with who struggle the most, and who have the most difficulty overcoming mental health issues, learning difficulties, gender identity issues, or otherwise, are the students whose parents are unsupportive or who don't try to understand or listen or (in some cases) who even go so far as to reject their child. The feeling of being rejected causes more damage than any disability or potential disorder that they might have. Working with these students, or with a troubled friend or co-worker, and helping them through their issues, has always proven to be very difficult when the individual is facing hurts from their past. These are past situations where they felt rejected by peers or unloved by a parent. I am not blaming parents for everything, but they can certainly set a foundation.

My brother-in-law will roll his eyes when he hears me say "All you need is love," but I continue to stand by this. Let's be more descriptive though. Love is about unconditional acceptance. No matter what your child turns out to be like and no matter what difficulties they face—whether genetically caused or not—they need your love and support. They need their home to be somewhere safe, a place to come back to where there is no judgment but where there is room for them to grow, learn, and turn into the person that they are becoming. I don't want to confuse a lack of discipline, though, for love. The goal of discipline is about ensuring that your child is safe and that they understand the confines of the society that they live in. This will help them to thrive. Discipline is necessary, but that's not the same thing as insisting on your way, your plan, and your preconceived ideas about who you think your child should be.

Maybe in a way Daniel and I are blessed. We can't use the markers that other parents do that indicate how their baby/child/adolescent is developing. If we set our expectations to this benchmark, we risk feeling discouraged or maybe even disappointed. We will simply have to observe, support, and nurture.

"As long as Little T is happy!"

September 30, 2015

Blog Post; **"Need for Close Monitoring."**

Yesterday we went for a follow-up appointment at the Children's cardiology department. Our first appointment was back in July, so we had a lot of questions. There was nothing new to report; the abnormalities were still there and are a cause for concern but there were no new surprises which was a relief. We have been anxious for this appointment in order to get a clearer picture of what to expect; also, the Children's is where I will deliver. Once Little T is born (hopefully after thirty-six weeks), we expect him/her to be in the hospital for a month minimum. He/she will need close monitoring and will likely have breathing difficulties.

Today at the Jewish General we had another ultrasound. There were three things that were noticed. There is more amniotic fluid than there should be. If this continues, they will do an amniocentesis to remove some fluid as the added pressure could pose a risk for me going into labour too soon. Also, in the brain they found a little bit more fluid than the last time. It is nearly above normal—but it is not there yet. Again, they will need to watch to make sure that it isn't increasing. Lastly, the heart is taking up a lot of space in the left lung, which could pose a problem as the lung develops. They want to proceed with caution by keeping an eye on these things. I will need to go for ultrasounds twice a week from this point forward.

Maria, the geneticist, was with us today during the ultrasound and she reassured us afterwards that the frequent appointments shouldn't be a cause of too much worry. They are just the doctors' way of keeping a close eye on things. They don't have any way to control the situation so evaluating it often is their way of keeping on top of it..

Since the buildup of amniotic fluid could cause an early labour, it was felt that I needed to look at whether I should continue working or not. Being on my feet and having the extra weight could cause early labour. Dr. Abenhaim, my doctor, said that it was okay for me to work part time for the next two weeks, but that I then should stay off work. I'm okay with this as it will give me time to finish up some things at work before I go.

Over the next weeks they will monitor how the baby continues to develop and if his/her lung or brain development is at risk. If so, they may need to consider inducing me before the thirty-six weeks. This wouldn't be ideal for the baby's heart, which they want to be as strong as possible for the eventual surgery, but it would be a case of deciding what takes precedence.

Daniel and I are doing okay. It's always good to have the day together after these appointments. None of this is beyond what we were expecting. In any case, knowing we will have regular ultrasounds is comforting as we'll know on a continual basis how things stand. I wanted to keep you updated as time goes on.

October 11, 2015

Blog Post; **"Thanksgiving."**

It might seem strange to know that I've been thinking about all the things to be thankful for. But I think having a positive attitude has really helped us through the past few months. Gaining perspective allows us to look at the big picture of our individual situation, and to see that, although they are difficult, things aren't beyond hope. Taking things one day at a time is only possible by looking forward, not by focusing on what's wrong. By finding or creating things to laugh about and by taking advantage of what blessings have been given to us, we face each day with joy.

So . . . what follows is my list of what I'm thankful for.

Our recent ultrasounds show some stability; there has been no increase in amniotic fluid, and no increase in fluid in the ventricles, meaning that the left lung still has room to develop. So, the hope is that there will be no reason to force an early delivery.

We have ongoing regular visits at the Jewish General with an excellent team of high-risk pregnancy doctors and ultrasound technicians, a geneticist, and social workers. They take good care of us, and since we go regularly, this allows me some peace of mind; I worry less about what could be going wrong.

I am aware that having free access to health care throughout this whole process is a unique blessing. As a Canadian citizen, I never fully realized how blessed we really are. I did just a little bit of research and found out that to pay out of pocket for an ultrasound costs between one hundred and $1,000, depending on the length of time that the equipment is used and the specific type of technology. We have had roughly ten so far with top of the line technology, and we have many more to come. In addition, there are all the blood tests, genetic tests, etc. that we have undergone. We also know that Little T will be in the hospital for at least a month.

The cost for all of this is something that we don't have to worry about, leaving us free from the kind of stress that so many have to face when sickness, disease, or injury falls upon them. If Little T were to be born in a third-world country, sure, we might have the peace of mind of being completely unaware that something was wrong, but once he/she was born . . . I really don't like to think of how helpless we would feel . . . it would be an outcome that we would have no choice but to accept.

I am so thankful for you as listeners. I am thankful for your understanding, your interest in how we are doing, and your response to what we need. I am also thankful for the people around us—especially my work colleagues. Work does not have to be a worry, especially for me, and I am able to take time away from work, without financial stress, to rest and emotionally prepare.

I am thankful for the time, particularly the time that Daniel and I have together throughout all these medical visits, and the time we share with family and friends.

I am thankful for all the caring messages that we have received and for everyone who is praying for us. It lifts us up and encourages us. We will never again take for granted the loving, supportive communities that we have around us.

I am thankful that during the whole pregnancy, I have been doing well physically and emotionally. Hormones being hormones, they don't always run in every expectant mother's favour. Had I been feeling depressed, keeping perspective would not have been so easy for me, but neither would it have been for Daniel and the others around me. This way we can support each other; I can be there for him, as well as he for me.

I am thankful for all our moments with Little T. I feel pokes and thumps, and Daniel and I have little talks with him/her. Daniel shares hockey news and facts in order to educate another future Canadiens fan. I like to share my favorite songs and my hopes and fears. Our extended family also likes to share how excited they will be to meet Little T.

I am thankful for the gift of becoming a mother and for the many role models whom I have around me. I am feeling thankful that I will have many wise women to seek advice from. Both my mother and my mother-in-law are wonderful examples to me. I am feeling blessed as well to have friends and family from whom I can seek advice.

I am thankful for Daniel and the person he is. For over thirteen years now we have continued to grow and laugh together. I am thankful because I know that he will be a wonderful father to our child. I am thankful for my father and Daniel's father who continue to show us what it means to have pride and joy in your children.

I am thankful that we have already come this far. There is only a month and a half to go; we have come further than our worst fears would have predicted.

I am thankful that so much planning has already been done by the Jewish General and the Children's to ensure that the best medical care is given to Little T leading up to and after he/she is born.

I am thankful that Daniel and I can hold on to a sense of peace. We realize that worrying or making attempts to control any outcomes will simply leave us feeling depleted, frustrated, or hopeless. We are holding on to a peace that surpasses all understanding.

October 28, 2015

Blog Post; **"The Hurry and the Wait."**

Little T and I had our first disagreement. Apparently Little T thought that arriving early was a good idea; this led to a very long day at the hospitals on Monday.

Maybe Little T just took Grandma too literally when on Sunday afternoon, at a shower with some friends and family, she presented a cake which said, "I'm coming out." Grandma also insisted that Diana Ross's catchy song of the same name be played as we cut the cake.

Whatever it was, at 4:00 a.m. the next morning I woke up from a lousy sleep of tossing and turning. I was feeling very uncomfortable no matter what I did. I proceeded to the living room where I tried once again to get some sleep. Eventually I played some relaxing audio tracks of ocean waves and I focused on relaxing different areas of my body. The funny thing was, as relaxed as I was everywhere else, my stomach kept tightening no matter what I did. I figured it was probably time to do a little research on what contractions were. I felt a little silly when I learned that they didn't always come with pain. This was an assumption that I had made about early labour signs that I'd garnered from many TV shows or movies. This meant that I had been getting contractions for the last few weeks, but I had just figured that Little T had developed the strange habit of wanting to flex all his/her muscles at the same time.

Calmly, I started to track how frequently the contractions were happening. When I realized that they were happening every five minutes or less, I began to prepare myself for a hospital visit. I waited until the more reasonable hour of 6:00 a.m. to text my parents and to gently wake Daniel. I told him that we might need to make a trip to the hospital, and, in case we did, he would benefit from a shower before going. When 7:00 a.m. rolled around, the contractions hadn't let up, so my parents came by to pick us up. Daniel later said, "At that moment, seeing your parents arrive, I finally realized that oh, this is happening." Off we went to the hospital, my dad joking that this was all a ploy my mom had cooked up to get a lift to work.

I was told that if I was going into labour, I would have to deliver at the Royal Victoria Hospital to be at the site of the Children's Neonatal Unit. Figuring that this was still not actual labour, we decided to go to the Jewish General where our case was known and where they could properly assess what was going on. In the worst case scenario they could remove some amniotic fluid which might have been causing the contractions.

When we arrived at the case (delivery) unit, we were greeted by our doctor with a kind and inquisitive "Hi guys, what are you doing here?" How nice it was to be greeted by a familiar face. He set us up with a nurse, and soon I was in a hospital room with both my contractions and the baby's heartbeat being monitored. I was barely dilated, but the contractions weren't letting up so my doctor presented us with the option of being transferred by ambulance to the Royal Vic either right away, or without rush in two hours if the contractions still weren't letting up by then. We opted for the calmer process, so they prepared all the paperwork that was needed in order to transfer our case. By 10:00 a.m. I was at the Royal Vic, with Little T's heartbeat and my contractions being monitored once again.

I started to get a bit of lower back pain and the contractions now showed some spiking so the thought was that this might be the day; I was transferred into a birthing room. The hours dragged on. Into the afternoon the contractions started to decrease in intensity and frequency, but at times they would go back up again. We eventually saw one of the neonatal doctors; he wanted to make sure that we understood the process and what would happen with Little T upon birth, depending on his/her condition and ability to breathe on his/her own. He emphasized that the longer that Little T stayed in the womb, the more time the lungs would have to develop and get stronger. Maybe that was what I needed to hear, or what Little T needed to hear, because a few hours afterwards, the contractions decreased again.

At 8:00 p.m., since I hadn't dilated anymore, one of the high-risk pregnancy doctors said that I was okay to go home. She gave us further instructions on when to call or come in again due to signs of labour and contractions. She said that the focus was now on resting at home and trying to prolong the delivery for as many days as possible. Just like that we were back at home—exhausted but greatly relieved.

Monday night through Tuesday I was constantly shifting from sleeping or napping, to being wide awake and watching TV. I was still having contractions but realized that adjusting how I was sitting or lying could help to calm them. Even though the doctor hadn't officially put me on bed rest, I figured that it was wise to impose it on myself. Tuesday night I had a full night's sleep and on Wednesday Daniel stayed home. We took it easy all of Wednesday, and I had barely any contractions.

Maybe the whole experience on Monday hadn't been about Little T taking the cue to come out, but rather had been a message for me that I really needed to rest and put my feet up. The previous Monday had been my last day of work, so from Tuesday onwards I had been at home. Yes, I relaxed and watched TV, but I also organized, sorted, and took Laska, our dog, for walks. I figured that all was good. Little T had time, and so did I, to get things ready.

Or maybe Little T had wanted to make sure that we were all familiar with the new surroundings at the Royal Vic and the Children's, since that was where we needed to end up eventually. I had also gotten a chance to test what I had packed in my hospital bag and to re-evaluate what I really needed for the actual main event. I knew now what to expect from the Birthing Centre and I had met one of the doctors from the Neonatal Intensive Care Unit. Leaving the hospital

Monday night, I joked to my sister that it had all been just a very long intake meeting. On Monday it was made official that we would continue any follow up at the Royal Vic from now on. More on that later, as Thursday was a big day of follow-up appointments plus a cardiology visit.

Well, I sincerely hope that there is still time before Little T makes another attempt at his/her big appearance. Friday will be the thirty-six week marker. That was the amount of time that the cardiologist had first said that we should make it to, in order to ensure Little T's best chance of being strong enough for an eventual heart surgery. More time, even days, would help Little T to become stronger. For me, it would allow things to fully sink in. I could properly learn that resting is a very important way to take care of myself. Being rested would also help me to take care of Little T.

October 29, 2015

An Email to Family and Close Friends.

Hi,

Today was a long and very full day. The ultrasound showed that my amniotic fluid has gone up again, but other than resting there is nothing to be done about that. I'm just hoping that this doesn't induce labour. The ventricle sizes are a little above normal, but again, we are so close to delivery that there wasn't much emphasis placed on that. They noticed a slight shortness in length of a few of the baby's bones (femur and tibia), but there were no signs that they appeared abnormal, so they weren't worried at all as it was the first time that this had been seen. I did a stress test again (as I did on Monday), and my contractions and the baby's heart rate were also monitored again. The baby's heart rate was normal. I am still having contractions, but they aren't intensifying, which is good.

We had a cardiology ultrasound as well and met with the other main cardiologist, Dr. Jutras. They think they might know why there is a hole between the aorta and the pulmonary artery. This doesn't really change much. When the baby has surgery, all the abnormalities will be addressed. The cardiologist basically suggested that Little T will need respiratory support right away after birth. Surgery may happen sooner, depending on how the baby is doing. If surgery occurs before three months, then another one will probably be needed within the first year since he/she will grow so much and grow out of the replacement valve, etc. that they put in.

The cardiologist said that he thought I would need a C-section but when we saw the high-risk pregnancy doctors soon after, they were clear that they would rather I have a natural birth. They will be monitoring the baby and I closely and will make the decision then if they feel that the baby is better off having a C-section. Having a natural birth will help the baby's lungs develop properly. My new doctor basically said that the cardiologist wasn't an OBGYN and so it wasn't their call.

We also visited the Neonatal Intensive Care Unit (NICU) and were shown around. We asked questions and spoke to the head doctor of the unit. It was good to see what we can expect. They encourage parent involvement, and the good thing is that the high-risk delivery room is right down the hall from the NICU ever since the two hospitals merged. Thus, Daniel will be able to go straight away to see the baby and whenever I am able, I will follow. The difficult news, for all of you, was when we learned that there are no visitors allowed in the NICU except the babies' parents. When Little T goes for surgery, the recovery room in cardiology will be a different story, but for protection of the babies and for parent privacy, the NICU is very strict on their no visitors policy.

Everyone was very nice and supportive today. The

cardiologists are always grimmer to meet, but I was glad we didn't finish with them today. Instead, the last person that we met with was our new obstetrician who was very hopeful. We go back next Monday and Thursday for another stress test and to check my amniotic fluids.

I didn't sleep much last night and am feeling physically and emotionally drained. I don't really want to talk tonight. I just need to rest.

Love you all,

Liz

SECTION 2

What to do with Waves of Grief?

Water

tranquil
fluid
changing but beautiful in every moment
disappearing movement

the sounds may be rushing,
or delicate droplets
splashes when I first dip in
outside voices are muffled when I submerge myself in it

movement allows for a feeling of being carried
I am lifted upwards
prevented from sinking
as long as I let myself go, not panic, and relax into its
presence

waves from a distance are beautiful
and yet being in them can be terrifying
feeling one coming without knowing how to escape
fearfully waiting
flinching
then . . .
pull and push
I am being moved and washed over
recovering and finding my footing again
standing up

seeing where I landed
realizing I am okay
maybe a little scratched and weakened
but much less than I feared
now . . .
anticipating the next wave
but this time the fear has subsided

Grief follows its own set of rules. There is no knowing when it will come or when it will subside. It is triggered by the memories of very personal circumstances. No matter how much time has passed, no one knows what you are going through. It's a private tidal wave of emotions. You can spend a lot of energy hiding this. It is a very personal pain that often comes unexpectedly. So we mask it from others—sometimes for very good reasons.

Grief is just like water pressure. It can build and build until it is finally released. I find that when I'm in a pool, a shower, or a bath, or when I'm caught outside on a rainy day that these are perfect times for me to allow tears of sadness or grief to flow. I have found a great release in these times.

Your path led through the sea, your way through the mighty waters, though your footprints were not seen. Psalms 77:19 (New International Version)

In my own experience with grief, I have had trouble seeing God carry or comfort me through it. As this verse suggests, I did not see his footprints alongside me. Maybe it was because I wasn't walking on the beach while safely watching the beauty of the waves from afar. I was in the water and being tossed around by the waves. I was trying to catch my footing—if only for a moment—before another wave came along. But that new wave would dash me back into the surf. I was crashing into the shoreline and being pulled back in. When my battle with grief was at its worst, that was always when I avoided it the most. I was afraid that it would completely take over, sweep me under, and take me too deep to be found. I would drown in essence in the pain that accompanied it. Yet, I physically felt the urge to be in water and to be completely surrounded by it.

Maybe that's where God was too. In the deep, mighty waters.

From November 2, 2015, to July 2016 I began my grieving process. I was off work from November through to the end of February, and I was able to explore grief through ceramics, music, writing, and being in water. My optimism from my Christian faith was still a big part of how I chose to see the loss that I had experienced. My blog posts were much less frequent. In between posts I would journal, but I kept these thoughts to myself due to the highly personal nature of my reflections, and also my need at the time to keep others from seeing the intense thoughts and emotions that I was having. I was not always comfortable with the form that grief would take, and I was trying to manage this myself.

November 8, 2015

Blog Post; **"Not for the Faint of Heart."**

Theodore a.k.a. Little T Bartlett

We asked Little T to make it to thirty-six weeks and he did. He fought hard and so did we. We never gave up on each other. Little T passed away peacefully; we aren't exactly sure when, but somewhere between Sunday night and Monday morning, November 2.

Daniel and I had gotten up on Monday morning to head to a follow up doctor's appointment at the Royal Vic. It was going to be another stress test, and my contractions were to be monitored as well as the baby's heartbeat. They couldn't find his heartbeat right away but thought that they had it at some moments. However, it was just jumping between his and mine. They decided that it would be clearer if they did an ultrasound. Immediately the doctors saw that there was no longer a heartbeat or any movement. Little T had peacefully passed away.

We asked to be transferred back to the Jewish General for the delivery the same day. Tuesday evening, around 10:00 p.m., Daniel and I and members of our families were able to finally hold him. The delivery was long, but I won't remember it as being difficult but rather the time when I felt the love and support of our families the most. My mom and dad, Devon[3] and his girlfriend, S.P., Meaghan[4], Daniel's parents, Debbie and Ken, John, Daniel's cousin, and of course Daniel were all there with their unwavering support. For the delivery, my mom, Meaghan, Debbie, and Daniel stayed with me and supported me physically by dampening my brow with a cold compress, and holding my hand.

There were even funny moments throughout, and the many nurses and doctors were extremely supportive. They did their best to make me comfortable—yes, lots of pain meds. I didn't think about it much but knew that I just had to get through it. At the end, I would be able to hold Little T, and that's all I focused on.

It was such a blessing to watch family hold him in their arms. I think he made it this far to allow people that chance. He wasn't that small after all. It was touching to see his face and nose and little mouth. He had the Bartlett nose and chin. He had big "little feet" which didn't come as a surprise as I had felt them kick all the time.

We have no regrets but remain thankful for the time that we had together and to have had the chance to hold him. After the delivery, the doctors said that in the end it had been the placenta that had detached. It wasn't Little T's heart that had given up, but rather something outside of any of our control. We take comfort in knowing that to the end, Little T kept

[3] Devon is my youngest brother.

[4] Meaghan (Meg) is my older sister.

fighting and was strong. We did the most we could have done. We take comfort in knowing that he didn't have to struggle and that we didn't see him struggle. Had he made it through the delivery, there were other issues present, including kidney and brain swelling. He would have been rushed off to the Children's where he probably would have awaited the same fate, though perhaps not immediately—but we still would have expected it to have happened soon after.

On Tuesday evening, my pastor, Nick Brotherwood, took some time with us, with Little T, and the family. He led us in some prayers together for Little T. It was a meaningful moment and how I think Little T would have liked it. We will not be holding a service or memorial. For us, that was our service. We know that so many of you were holding us and Little T in your hearts and lifting us up in prayer. We ask you to continue. Little T lived for thirty-six weeks in our hearts and will continue to do so.

Daniel and I are doing reasonably okay. Time together and time with family and friends who stop by has been nice and helpful. People's kind gestures of words, flowers, and food are really appreciated. We don't mind at all being contacted directly; we read your kind words at our own pace. Carrying on with some normalcy is nice. Like before, we are finding things to laugh about every day and we do feel up to hanging out with friends. As usual, we want to hear what is going on in your lives.

Emotions come at us in waves. Sometimes they are little ones that pass in a few minutes, and sometimes they feel like tidal waves that wipe us out completely. We remind each other, as we have been doing since July, to take things one day at a time.

I am not feeling up to leaving the house much just yet, but appreciate people stopping in. I will be off work for a while and am finding ways to take care of myself and to process everything that has happened. Daniel returns to work tomorrow but will have more time now that he has dropped his university class. Meaghan is still living with us and is a huge support to have around. John is next door, and my parents are just a ten minute walk away. Debbie and Kenny and Greg, Daniel's brother, are a short drive away. Jeff[5], Daniel's brother, and Devon are just a phone call away. We remain well supported by so many people and are so grateful for this.

Some people have asked if they could honour Little T by donating to his memory. We aren't sure yet where this could be done. I want to talk to Rodrick in Malawi about the possibility of opening a fund for prenatal care. The fund would allow women in the village to be transported to the local hospital for prenatal visits and for the delivery. Warm Heart Initiatives is the name of the organization. I will keep you up to date.

I may continue to write, and I may not. It depends on how it helps me to process things.

Thank you again for all of your support. You have helped to carry us through all of this.

Emails from my mom to friends and family after Little T's passing and birth.

From: Darlene Johnstone

Date: Nov. 4, 2015 12:41 PM

Subject: **Dearest Family and Friends**

This is a letter of love, sadness, relief, and thankfulness for all of you, as we have together faced the journey of Theodore (Little T).

---

[5] Jeff is Daniel's brother.

Thank you so much for your love, kindness, and support. We are resting in an unexplainable peace for now, cradled in a bigger love than all of us, as we continue to support Liz and Daniel.

My fears and prayers were for Theo (Little T) to enter safely into the world and to our awaiting arms. In fact, he entered in peace, his precious heart having stopped in utero sometime on Monday morning. He has been, and continues to be, loved by all of us.

Meg, Debbie, and I were privileged to be a part of the birthing process, and it was such an honour and grace to do so, and to witness the tenderness and love between Daniel and Liz through it all and also to witness Lizzy's formidable strength—physical, as well as emotional and spiritual.

We couldn't be prouder of Meaghan, who lovingly nursed and supported Liz through the long and exhausting process. She is a priceless jewel, forged in the fires of life . . . a blessing to her sister and brother-in-law, and to us all. Her tenderness, grace, thoughtfulness, and humor shone through the whole experience. Please continue to surround her with your love, prayers, and support. I know her tender heart is breaking with grief for her sister's loss and for Daniel.

Devon is with us, strong and tender, loving and supportive through every step, despite the distance and his hectic schedule. We are so proud of him, and awed by his intelligence and devotion to his research and career in gestational genetics. He, more than any of us, may contribute to our larger understanding.

Dave has stood by us all with tremendous strength and hope .. and with tears of sorrow and pride. He has kept the wheels on the bus in so many servant-like ways, supporting his little girls and Dan, Devon, and I in ways practical and emotional, seen and unseen. Watching him hold little Theo in his arms reminded me of the loving father that he has always been. Theo will know his amazing grandpa from another plane, and indeed know and love us all with a pure spirit. He is now with the Great Father, the one who longs to embrace us and fold us into his safe strong arms, and who offers a comfort that we so need right now.

Debbie, Daniel's mom, was there with us . . . she was loving, gentle, and radiant with kindness and concern. Watching her tenderly wipe Lizzy' s brow, bring water, and support Daniel through words, thoughts, and gentle deeds, truly blessed my heart. Sharing with her our worries and hopes as grandmothers, each of who wants to protect their children and their child and do whatever she can in her helplessness, makes me love and appreciate her more than ever.

Kenny, Daniel's dad, paced with the best of us, took care of us with food and coffee, cried with us, and spent sleepless nights keeping watch. He and Debbie love Lizzy as their own daughter and it shows now as much as ever.

Cousin John, a next-door neighbor to Liz, Dan, and Meg shared this roller coaster ride with us. His humor and his sweetness have embodied the wonderful qualities of all the friends and family who have and will continue to stand by us. Liz and Dan have an amazing community of friends, as do we.

Today we rest, shed some tears, and enjoy this beautiful new day—now stronger as a family united by the strangest of experiences. We will find our way, separately and together, and with you, our loving family and friends.

Thank you.

I started to write a journal for myself on November 10th 2015. Its purpose was to write down thoughts and emotions I was processing for myself and feelings I needed to keep close and not share. I knew that some of these thoughts and emotions were darker. They were things that I didn't feel comfortable sharing with others. I didn't want the complication of dealing with people's reactions. When I was a teenager, I would write in a journal. Sometimes it was poems, and sometimes it was thoughts and feelings as they came to me. I hadn't done so since my youth. I felt I needed an outlet, so I started again..

November 10, 2015

Journal Entry

I miss him. I miss him kicking. As uncomfortable as being pregnant can sometimes be, I miss it. I was supposed to be still at home—like I am now. Little T, kicking in my belly while I try to stay relaxed to ward off contractions that are too intense. I was supposed to be getting ready for frequent hospital visits. Instead, I am at home, and I feel lonely and bored.

At some moments it seems that I am fortunate to have the time to recover physically and emotionally and to do the things that I love, like pottery, and music, etc. I also do things for Malawi and work, and research anxiety management techniques. At other moments, it feels so daunting to have this much time—to be swimming in it. There's too much time to think or feel lonely. I don't want to be hanging on to the moment when Daniel gets home—but—I do want to spend all my time with him and be near him.

My love, my love,

all that we have been through.

The strength that you have shown me.

The forever patient and joyful attitude you carry.

You help me with each day.

You help me keep on.

My love, my love,

the things that we have hoped for.

The heartbreak of losing him.

Sharing it with you eases the pain.

You help me with each day.

You help me keep on.

My love, my love,

deciding together to focus on the good.

To cherish the love shown by those around.

I could not have seen it this way without you.

You help me with each day.

You help me keep on.

My love, my love,

you are God's greatest gift to me.

The strength I have you help me to sustain.

With no room for blame we made room for joy.

You help me with each day.

You help me keep on.

My love, my love.

November 17, 2015

Journal Entry

I am okay with seeing toddlers and kids, but seeing babies is so hard. It started after we found out about Little T's health concerns. I wasn't giving up on him—I was just trying to take things one step at a time. The furthest that I could imagine and hope for at that time was to see Little T as a baby. A week before his death I was in a breastfeeding café/shop looking for tank tops. I couldn't bear being in there long. It was too hard to face that I might never get to the point with Little T where he would be healthy enough to be out of the hospital, never mind imagining that we would one day be able to go out together, with him strapped to me, and be around other normal moms.

My close girlfriend Sarah is expecting her baby soon. She was scheduled to give birth three weeks after me. It's hard to see her pregnant, and know that she can feel her baby move. I don't want this to be between us and I want to keep seeing her. She has two young kids already, one who is three and a half and another who is one year and seven months. I love those little kids and seeing them brings me a lot of joy. As well, I am really anxious to see Jeff's kids, my niece and nephew in Vancouver who are now four and three. I just want to be around them as they are very much a part of our lives. It's something special to see them grow up. But, because they live far away, we're missing out on that which is hard. You'd think that Little T's passing would make it harder for me to see them grow and develop little personalities. But it brings me comfort and joy. I like to be a part of their lives.

I don't know how I am going to be when I see Sarah with her newborn, and hear about how it went in the hospital. I really hope it's not a boy. For some reason I think that that would make it easier for me to not compare, and to be happy for her and her husband.

I don't know how I feel about having another child. Especially during the first week, probably with hormones and all, I was ready to be instantly pregnant again. What I really wanted, though, was to be eight months pregnant again, and to be getting ready to give birth to Little T. I wouldn't even have changed any of his health concerns, because everything that we knew about him was part of who he was to us. All of the medical appointments helped to shape in our minds the image of who our child was and would be. Little T had a very big heart, but one with health issues that would have needed surgeries. Any other baby without such concerns would not have been our Little T and I wouldn't have traded him for that. He was perfect to me—to us.

I must remind myself that he didn't experience any pain or discomfort, and that had he been born, he would have. He was spared from that. Although we wish so much to have had more time with him, he was better off this way. I did see him as a baby, though. I saw his little nose and his little feet, but I didn't get to dress him or change him. I didn't get to see him wiggle or cry. And I didn't experience the joy of being a mother that others do.

I don't really know how this grief thing works. What I presume is that grief is just a period that you go through. It takes you over completely for a time and then lifts its hold on you. That hasn't been my experience so far. At some moments it's been more like little waves—say if someone brings it up, or I see or hear something that brings the memory flooding back. Thoughts sometimes come to mind without order or reason. Some days I wake up fine— others I don't. Some days are normal and good, and others aren't but I can still describe them as good even though I feel a lot of pain and sadness.

Some moments I want to feel the pain and I look to be reminded of him. Other moments I want to feel something else, but I don't need to push the thoughts out if they come, they just come less intensely. I think everyone must experience grief in their own way. I am very fortunate to have people around me, and to have an incredible love for Daniel that provides a break from the sadness. It's a funny time to say it, but it's the time in my life when I have felt the most in love. Our love for each other never faded, but I suppose that, because right now all of our emotions are so raw, the love we feel for each other has intensified. Being around Daniel just lifts me up and I think that that has spared me from completely falling on my face through all of this.

Acceptance, I think, has been an easier process for us simply because we knew in July that his death was a very possible outcome. I remember reflecting on this and deciding that I was going to cherish every day with him in my belly as I didn't know how many days we might have once he was born.

November 22, 2015

Journal Entry

I will always be a mother. It's not about looking forward to it again. I still am. It pains me more to think that I am no longer a mother than to dwell on the fact that I am one. I look forward to becoming a mother again, for a new opportunity, but not as a replacement or substitute. No one can take the place of Little T or change the fact that he was our first child. That would feel like a dishonour to his memory. All of my first sensations of being pregnant and being a mother were experienced by and through him.

December 5, 2015

Journal Entry: **On the Plane Ride to Vancouver.**

As soon as I got the medical clearance that I was healing fine physically, Daniel and I booked a trip out west to see his brother, Jeff, Jeff's fiancé , and their two kids for a couple of weeks. We will spend a week with them in Chilliwack, British Columbia, and then the two of us will spend a couple of days in Seattle, Washington.

Before booking, Daniel asked if it was too soon for me to be away from the safety and privacy of home. It was a big first step. It would be the first trip where I would be far away from the apartment, the place I felt I had shared so much space and time with Little T. Last night I had another uncontrollable episode of crying while packing. I didn't know what and how much to pack of Little T's keepsakes from the hospital. I also found leaving the physical space of the apartment a sort of betrayal, as if I was leaving Little T behind. His ashes would remain in the apartment in a pottery piece that I had made.

I just finished watching an in-flight film called Mr. Holmes. It was a sweetly surprising film about the gift of understanding and how human intellect is not enough. The movie is about the grief of a mother who has suffered two miscarriages and was then told that she should no longer try to have a baby due to the health risks. Her husband all the while is dismissing her grief.

Holmes was hired to follow her and to find out where she would disappear to during the day. Even Sherlock Holmes couldn't see her deep pain and loneliness. He couldn't offer her the companionship and understanding that she was seeking. There is something very powerful and intimate about feeling understood by another person. It is the power of no longer feeling alone.

What a gift it is to have people around me, and most of all my love, my companion. He is willing to understand my grief and not judge me for it, even though he does not feel things the same way that I do. He is not reminded in the way that I am of that which is not. There have been reminders on the plane ride: I heard strangers talk about their children, I panicked because I didn't want to sit next to a baby, and I saw a woman who was pregnant. The grief and inner trauma welled up— yet I had to pretend outwardly that I wasn't feeling the pain—that I wasn't missing Little T with a sadness beyond description.

December 16, 2015

Journal Entry: **Arriving Back Home in Montreal.**

Visiting Jeff, Sasha, Jack, and Audrey, whom we couldn't see during all the events leading up to and when Little T passed, was very therapeutic. We didn't talk about Little T much. It was just a few moments in the car between me and Jeff. I never talked about it with the kids, who were then three and four. Jack and Audrey never asked about the baby, but months ago they had been so excited about having a little cousin.

The six of us shared an early Christmas morning together. We experienced for the first time The Elf on the Shelf and its magic for children. (We also observed the creative angst it produced in parents who needed to find new locations every evening.) We went to see The Good Dinosaur with Jack and Audrey. Poor three-year-old Jack cried and cried when the friends went their separate ways at the end of the movie. We went on excursions to secondhand bookstores, took car rides into Vancouver, and read bedtime stories. One night we babysat the kids while my brother-in-law and sister-in-law were out together. When I put my nephew to bed and watched him sleep, grief swept over me. I could see the family resemblance between my nephew and Little T. It was very heavy, and I cried uncontrollably.

During the trip I rarely pulled out his keepsakes and the physical change of environment did me good. Although the night I put my nephew to bed was extremely painful, I was still glad that I came. I remember not wanting to lose out on moments that would help to build our relationship. The time we had together, when it was just us two, with Daniel getting a break from work, was especially wonderful. It helped to solidify us. We continued to build memories when the two of us visited Seattle as we had visited the city together on a previous trip. We went to the public market and enjoyed a drink together at a pub. On the drive from Chilliwack to Seattle we listened to The National in the car. Every time I hear it now, I think of that drive, and it is a happy memory.

December 19, 2015

Journal Entry

Meg and I went to a Patrick Watson concert yesterday. It was magical. Carried by the music and the creative display of lights and sounds, I was transported somewhere else entirely. A Montreal concert crowd is the surefire ticket to lift you to somewhere else. After the concert, Patrick Watson went into the street with his homemade megaphone instrument. We stuck close to the crowd that surrounded him, feeling giddy to be so close to such a brilliant musician. It was as though we had stumbled upon a truly unique moment by accident!

December 23, 2015

Blog Post; **"Why Would I Celebrate Christmas?"**

To my readers who share my Christian faith, I have been asking myself many questions about what role faith has played after the year I've had. This is especially true considering the personal pain that Daniel and I and our families have suffered, and what has been happening in the world around us—in Syria[6], in Paris[7], and in so many other places on our

---

[6] The civil war in Syria continued in 2015. People were forced out of their homes, and many fled their country. The Syrian refugee crisis is still ongoing today

[7] On the evening of November 13, 2015, a series of terrorist attacks occurred in Paris, France. According to Britannica.com, 130 people died and more than 350 were injured.

troubled Earth. Do I really want to focus on the traditional Christmas story and the events of a baby being born so long ago? It is a painful reminder of what Daniel and I have lost.

This year in preparation for Christmas, I turned my attention to the book of Isaiah[8]. Apparently, Isaiah's focus was to analyze the failures of all the nations around him, and he pointed to a future Messiah who would bring peace.

"Surely he took up our infirmities and carried our sorrows." Isaiah 53:4 (New International Version)

"They shall obtain joy and gladness, and sorrow and sighing shall flee away." Isaiah 35:10 (New Revised Standard Version)

"Behold, the virgin shall conceive and bear a Son, and shall call His name Immanuel, [God is with us]." Isaiah 7:14 (English Standard Version)

"God has given us a son . . .

His name will be Wonderful Counselor, Mighty God, Everlasting Father, Prince of Peace." Isaiah 9:6 New King James Version (NKJV))

Of the four gospels, the book of John is my favourite account of Jesus's life. At Christmas we may be focusing on His birth, but really we are joyously thinking of what He brings into this world—and into our own lives—as the following Scriptures show.

"I have come that they may have life, and that they may have it more abundantly. John 10:10" (New King James Version)

As I have allowed myself to fully feel the grief and sadness, being open to my emotions has also allowed me to be open to the great joy, laughter, and love that I have shared with those around me.

---

[8] Isaiah is a book in the Bible found in the Old Testament. This is before Jesus comes into the story which is in the New Testament.

"I am the light of the world. He who follows Me shall not walk in darkness, . . . " John 8:12 (New King James Version)

There is a hope that can be found in following Christ. His life is the greatest example of showing love and forgiveness. He leaves no room for bitterness, but instead performs acts of kindness. He demonstrates understanding. He transforms people's lives so that they can carry on these same acts in this world, acts that bring light and joy and prevent us all from walking in solitude and darkness.

"The light shines in the darkness, but the darkness has not understood it." John 1:5 (New International Version)

Although it is deeply painful, we have not been left alone in the darkness. Friends have come to us with understanding, kindness, and love. They have brought light that has lifted us through sorrow.

This Christmas, let us be a witness to the light that we experience in our own lives and be sure to share it with others.

Reflections on December 24, 2015

After having written the blog post above, I attended a Christmas Eve service but could not remain for the entirety of it. The songs about a baby being expected were too much to bear and I left the building before anyone could see me tear up. I gave the explanation that I had a family dinner to get to. This might have been the first sign of how, in person, I would push away grief to hide it from others. I also wanted to preserve the idea that I was a guidepost for others, especially in matters of faith, and an example of holding on to hope. My blog post was about showing others that grief doesn't need to pull you down to the point of despair. I thought that sharing about my grieving would be meaningful to others. That it had a purpose. I was unable to let others take care of me. I think if I had teared up in the service, I would have been cared for by those around me. In that moment, I did not want to take away from their Christmas experience and make it about me.

January 17, 2016

Blog Post; **"A New Year."**

On New Year's Day we said good riddance to 2015 and welcomed a brand-new year, a year ideally that would have less pain and many blessings. And yet now I wish for 2015 again. I want to go through it all over again just so I can be with Little T once more and spend a little more time with him.

Acknowledging this new year and the new beginnings has brought a sad realization. Little T's story is over. There are no more medical appointments. There are no more ultrasounds, showers, or baby books or toys to look at in the stores. The motherhood that I was planning for so long has gone. It was taken from me. We are no longer getting sympathy cards acknowledging his life. Things are moving on for everyone. Friends have had their babies and their stories are continuing. But the story of our parenthood isn't. All is at an end.

Daniel has started his master's degree in English literature full time, and I am involved in a new pottery studio, baking, singing and playing guitar, swimming, doing mindfulness meditations, and planning anxiety workshops for school. Having these things to occupy my time and thoughts is good, even healthy I suppose, because I can't really relive 2015. I can't go back in time and change what happened. But I also feel a strange sense of guilt. A feeling that I owe it to him, to Little T, to act like I am continuing to be his mother.

I just can't figure out what to do with that feeling. It has nowhere to go. I really can't fathom ever becoming pregnant again with another child—because I simply want to be pregnant again with Little T. I don't know if that feeling will ever change. I don't know if I can emotionally face being a mother to another child. I wonder if I'm even able. Am I strong enough to deal with the motherly worry of creating a new life? It was so painful dealing with it for eight months. It was a particular circumstance, but still it was real and will be a part of me forever.

You will find that I don't talk much about Little T anymore. I don't tend to bring it up and not many people really ask—at least not specifically. I think it's hard for me to see people who are worried or sad for me. My empathy gene kicks in, which is quite hyperactive most of the time anyways. I can't handle worrying for others right now, and seeing them in pain because I am in pain makes it all the harder. My own grief is manageable; handling other people's grief or concern for me isn't. I don't know if that makes sense, but it's just the way it is for me. Maybe in a way it's a protective mechanism because I am trying to go through grief in a healthy way (whatever that means) so that people don't need to worry about me. I refuse to let myself slip into depression.

Daniel and I promised each other that we wouldn't leave the other alone to pick up the pieces. We would be strong for each other. But that doesn't mean we push away how we are feeling. We just won't let it take us over completely. Throughout all this we have allowed for other feelings and experiences as well. It might seem like things are back to normal and how they were a year ago. In a way they are. We do things we love with the people we love. Normal has changed for us though, but it's not visible to others. I don't think we have even quite figured it out.

Right now I find myself more prone to be irritable and impatient with people's greed, judgment, negativity, or selfishness. The world doesn't need that crap and I certainly don't right now. I suppose it's just confirmation that I need more time. I could use a rest from work, as having patience is a big part of my job. I also need more time to take care of myself. Grief, I suppose, still needs more of my attention. Sometimes it calls to me in the middle of the night with its demands. I am learning to give it what it needs, or else I fear it will get the better of me in the long run. It won't go away without my acknowledging it; it will just mask itself as something else, like maybe anger. Doing the things that I enjoy (including sleeping in) seems to help give me the necessary energy to face grief. Writing seems to help, too. Until next time.

Reflections

Looking back on January 2016.

I was happy to focus on new things in the new year and to feel like I was moving forward. I helped open a pottery studio and invested time and energy in purchasing and setting up the place. Time alone at the pottery studio also gave me a chance to connect physically with clay, while tears and sadness surfaced. Focusing my attention on the creative task at hand in between the intense feelings really helped. Centering, lifting, waiting, centering again, trimming, waiting, wiping, dipping, and cleaning were a procession of actions that distracted me while I was healing.

I picked up my guitar more than I had in a long time and Meg and I sang songs together. I took time for art and music, both things that I had always loved but that I had been neglecting for many years. I helped at our church with some secretarial work, with preparing PowerPoint presentations for Sunday, and with coordinating leaders. I still had this drive to care for others and also the need to help in some way despite the grief. I wanted to see the pottery studio be a success and help our church function well. All these things were welcome distractions so that I wasn't only focused on pain and loss.

My nights were often interrupted. That was when memories

*and thoughts would creep in. Sleeping in was a necessity.
Getting outside with Laska helped me get going for the day as
well.*

February 2, 2016

Journal Entry

It feels like it's getting harder for me. I think I've let my guard
down. I've stopped trying to be "okay" for other people's
sakes. I find myself remembering the painful moments—the
tough ones like finding out the truth at the first ultrasound,
being at the hospital when Little T's heartbeat could no
longer be found, and many others. I find it harder now to
be around Sarah and her new baby. It was okay, surprisingly,
when her daughter was first born. In fact, I went to see her
in the hospital on Christmas Eve. Now, however, it's more
painful than ever to hear her talk about how the baby is
growing so fast, or making cute cooing noises, and all the
things a new mother will say. At these moments it's okay; I
manage to numb my feelings. But as soon as I am alone, the
waves come at me without mercy. They never let up.

I feel fortunate to have had the privacy of the whole pottery
studio to myself during the last couple of weeks. It's a helpful
place to be. It's a place to create and to listen to podcasts on
grief or mindfulness meditations. Today I talked to Little T,
which I hadn't done since the fall. The space is good—hard
but good. I don't want to be talking to friends or family right
now about any of this. I just need to let out the thoughts
and feel the heavy emotions. I don't think there's any talking
this through though—at least not without the risk of seeing
people's faces as they react to my probably depressing words.
My close friend Kim told me that I need to accept people's
empathy as their expression of love towards me and towards
us. I understand that now. I realize that people don't need to
hear me speak about it or to see me cry. I know that we are
loved, and it makes us stronger. It really does.

Kim shared a thought that I will hold deeply in my heart forever. She asked me if going through this experience has allowed me to understand grief any better, and if it would help me to help others who grieve. I answered that yes, I think it has. She replied, "Then Little T's life will continue to have an impact on an endless number of people's lives through you." I really hope so. I want so much, like most parents I presume, for his life to make an impact—a beautiful one—on this world. He has impacted me greatly, and Daniel too.

We watched the movie Room today. It's about a mother who is held captive for seven years. During that time she has a son who is now turning five. It is about how she tries to protect him from the harsh reality of their lives in the "room" and once out, how she helps him grow accustomed to the real world while dealing with her own personal trauma. The movie, not surprisingly, hit me very hard. I figured it would and I had delayed seeing it for several months because of that.

What hit me the most was how the rest of the world did not know her son, and while they were in the room he was all that she had; he was her world. I couldn't help but connect that with the feelings that I had when Little T was in my belly for eight months. Only I could feel his presence to that extent. Only I had the daily worry of wanting the best for him while dealing with my own sadness. I may have even been going through a trauma—that of knowing he wasn't completely safe. Her son did get out, though, and he got to see the world and to meet his grandparents and even their pet dog. I wanted that so much for Little T. I wanted Daniel and I to be able to show him the world and the simple but important things like a wet kiss from Laska. I really grieve this, the "what might have been" moments that we were forever denied.

There was a beautiful moment in the film when the boy, knowing that his mother is struggling, cuts his hair (which he symbolizes as his strength) and gives it to her. It's what pushes her to carry on. I would like to think that Little T, as strong as he was and as far as he was able to make it to eight months, passed his strength on to us. We'll be okay. But we will never be completely okay, as there are so many experiences that we will miss out on. We wanted to show him the world and protect him from it (all at the same time) and we'll never have the chance to do that.

But having his strength will help carry us through.

February 3, 2016

Journal Entry

It feels so awful to have to write to Sarah and tell her I don't want to see her and her baby Elise right now. There's no nice way to say that. There's no way that doesn't hurt her and that doesn't put her in a place of feeling guilty, and that really sucks. She has no reason to feel bad just because her baby lived and mine didn't. I hate that going through this could have the power to create distance between me and others, and even with family. I feel right now that I don't want to be around them much. I am finding myself feeling irritable, and for no reason.

Sarah said to me afterwards when we saw each other again that I hadn't needed to give a reason if I had wanted the space. She said that I hadn't needed to find a way to say it to make her feel okay about it; I just should have done what I had needed to do and that would have been perfectly okay. I think I am learning, for the first time really, that I should make decisions for myself, for Daniel and I, and just make them. I shouldn't fret about how they will be received. That part is beyond our control.

I watched Sarah have three kids and have been watching them grow up. Sarah was my mommy friend—a friend who had kids when I didn't, and then the friend whom I was supposed to share becoming a mom with. She found out that she was pregnant with her daughter, her third child (the fourth after an ectopic pregnancy), a month after I found out that I was pregnant with Little T. We talked about spending my maternity leave by going to the park together, and hanging out on her couch, while both breastfeeding.

We had weekly nights together when we would have a cup of tea and whatever delicious baked goods she had made. We would sit in front of the TV and chat and sometimes watch a series. I saw her kids often before bedtime or for the late-night feeding.

Daniel and I didn't want kids for a long time. Then suddenly I did, and eventually he felt ready as well. It didn't happen right away. In my restlessness, my dear friend was always there. She was almost as excited as we were when we found out that I was pregnant for the first time. I know how deeply she was affected by Little T's struggling health. I know she prayed probably more than anyone for his healing. I know that it nearly crushed her when she learned of Little T's passing. At the time, she was a month and a half away from giving birth to her third. If anyone could understand the pain, it was probably her.

I tried hard to be strong and to remain in her life and keep seeing her and her kids. I went to the hospital and held her daughter the day she was born. It was the day before Christmas, just over a month after Little T had passed. It wasn't as hard as I thought it would be—at least not then. I really didn't want his death to take every joy and celebration away from me. I didn't want to lose friendships and to become isolated. We kept hanging out for a couple of months after Little T died as we usually did. I would go over to their house and see the kids going to bed, and then watch her nurse her new baby.

I would be able to hold it together until I left her house and walked home alone. But it was indeed too difficult. It was too painful, and I was finally starting to allow myself to make room for the anger I had.

Sarah knew, way before I did, that I couldn't keep on seeing her like this with her kids and especially with her new baby. She insisted on coming to my place after she had put the kids down (once the newborn was a few months old). She was the one "mommy friend" I had who I could bear being around. She brought us meals and hugged me and cried with me during the more difficult or reflective moments. She made sure that we didn't drift apart, even though I knew it was hard for her to see me—without my baby.

I feel very sad. It is a very complex sadness. I am angry now because we never got that year together of sitting in the park while both of us care for our babies and watch her two others play. I am not developing a relationship with her youngest. I feel that Sarah and I have been robbed of time together and of building and sharing memories. This is something I deeply regret.

I felt a great sense of gratitude to her all through this. Even when I couldn't bear to be close to her kids, Sarah stood by me. She made as much time for me as she could and cared for me—on top of her three. And I know she also felt sadness and worry for me. She didn't shy away from this. It would have been very easy to drift away completely. It was harder to stay close, but she did. I will be forever grateful. She was able to just be with me—whenever I was emotional.

February 14, 2016

Journal Entry

Today was hard for me. The lead up to today was hard.

Today I went to my friend Elissa's baby shower. This was not just any baby shower but one for my family friend who, about a year ago, had a memorial service and burial for her first child, a pre natal baby whose kidneys never developed in the womb. Now, a year later, they are welcoming another son. She should be giving birth any day now. I wanted to be better and stronger and to not have it affect me so much. If it was going to be for anyone, I wanted to be happy for her, and happy without any other feelings because I hope to be in her situation again sometime soon.

It shouldn't have hurt, but it really did. It was a baby shower for a boy, with gifts, streamers on the wall, and even a cake that my mom made herself. It was too reminiscent of only a few months ago. There were discussions about labour and mothers were talking about how long it would be until their babies would be born. At many moments I felt like the lump in my throat would choke me and that the tears I was holding back would just take over. Before the shower, I think one of the things that I dreaded most would be to hear people talk about their "first" child and "first" crack at parenting. The stories I built up in my head, though, were so much worse than being there myself and living it.

Elissa and her husband are welcoming their second child—their second son. How important it is for me to acknowledge that. She is very excited to be welcoming her new son, and to be showered with gifts. I think what people are really doing is showering her with love. Her grandmother made her blankets—plural—many, many blankets. It was humorous to see exactly how many. But I knew that it was because she had had two years to knit. Thomas, their first son, was supposed to have had those blankets. It wasn't mentioned out loud, but I had a short exchange with my friend's mom reflecting on this.

I wish it hadn't been so hard, but it was. I needed not just the courage to get through it, but I needed to wear a "mask" as well, though not for the others—for Elissa and for me. She was joyous in those moments, and it wouldn't have done me or her any good to change that. At another time we could cry together, but not then. I didn't want this moment to become about me and my pain. I wanted that to be just for me right now. At this moment I wanted to keep that emotion all to myself.

I was very happy that I went. I felt relieved that I could get through it, and I wanted to be strong for her and to support her in welcoming another new life into their family. At a certain point I didn't need to hold back tears anymore. I felt some peace and could talk about baby stuff such as what to get, what not to get, what I had, what I still had, and what I could lend her. I spoke to Little T later that night asking him if it was okay that I had lent out his stuff, but that I would make sure to get it back for when his younger brother or sister came along. I said, "Don't worry, it will stay in the family because Elissa has always been like a cousin to me, and we will be in each other's lives always." I don't think that Little T minded.

I don't know if it will last—if tomorrow or in a week I will still feel this as strongly. But I left the shower feeling deeply that I wanted another child. Not that it really happens like that, but that maybe I could become pregnant again. In fact, we are roughly at the year's mark of when we became pregnant with Little T. Maybe it would be nice to go through a new pregnancy at the same time of year as I did with Little T. In fact, I have all the appropriate maternity clothes by season. It seems like it makes sense.

I dreaded today and yet I faced it. I think I did well in the end. I really needed to cry afterwards and now I do again, but that's okay. I will leave space for that, too.

March 6, 2016

Journal Entry

I feel like I haven't written in a long while, yet I have been thinking a lot. I have had many thoughts race through my mind, but because I wasn't emotional, I felt that I didn't need to take the time to write them down. Some of these thoughts aren't present anymore, but I do remember them. I remember thinking that I was pushing people away and that I didn't like that. I didn't like who I was for needing space and for not wanting to be around people. It made me mad that grief, this tragedy that had happened to us, was also turning me into an irritable grump who cringed at the idea of someone touching me to show their support.

I have stopped going on Facebook altogether to avoid seeing birth announcements, or really anyone posting or celebrating anything about their children. I just get so angry and upset. Some people do try to reach out. They ask if we can get together, but I really have no energy to endure other moms. I will be sad that they are sad for me. Or I will be angry that they bring up their own kids.

After Little T passed, I consciously decided to not become like this, and I fought against it. Or so I thought.

I was worried that if I felt anger it would last for a long time. But now, just as quickly as it comes, it seems to fade away. Maybe it will come back and visit again. That will probably happen if I am overtired. But I am now feeling grateful that I took time away from people, especially those with kids. No one was offended or took it personally as I had feared. Our relationship didn't change because of my actions.

I didn't expect to feel the most emotionally fragile in February, which was the fourth month after Little T's death, but that's how it happened. Working, especially at that time, would have been next to impossible because a major part of my job is to take care of other people's emotional health. Only in February did I learn to have empathy for myself because of everything that I had gone through and to let down my need to care for others before myself. I did not want to cause people to worry or to see them in pain because of me.

It's still there, but I think I understand myself better. I can ask for what I need without feeling guilty. Because I am emotionally unavailable, I can say "no" to opportunities to lend a hand to others, or to spend time with them. I can plan time for myself to JUST BE! I don't think I have ever done that. Usually when I do something—even if it's art, music, or a helpful relaxation—I think, "Who will this be for? Who will benefit from this other than me?"

I now only have a few weeks left before going back to work. As if this was a normal time off, I worry that I didn't do what I should have done, and that I will be held accountable for that because I was still paid. I feel like I should have been productive in some way. I really am a slave driver sometimes—to myself. I can't even give myself the freedom and the responsibility of taking care of myself. It's as if that's not enough. However, during all this time, I have had a desire and a need for art, music, writing, and inspiring ideas to bring back to work, and that, I think, has made a huge difference in keeping my spirits up. It has been a break from the grief and it has also given me some good tools and venues to help me to process things.

February was also when I went with a close friend who is getting married to shop for bridesmaid dresses, as I am a bridesmaid. Earlier that week I had wanted to cancel going as I had been feeling sensitive and unable to see people. To be supportive I decided to go and ended up having a lovely time with all the girls—that is, until we had to try on the dresses.

I am feeling very uncomfortable these days with an inflated stomach. It didn't bother me the first couple of months because everything was so ripe, and this was to be expected. Three months after giving birth, though, your body is supposed to have gone back to normal, whatever that means, but mine is forever changed. Now I feel that being mistaken for being pregnant will really affect me. I don't mind it personally; I don't crave to be thin and "socially" attractive. I never felt ugly when I was pregnant and big. Now I do because I want to be pregnant again. Until I am, though, this body seems useless to me—it s an empty shell. I have been careful about the clothes that I wear because I don't want to have to think about someone noticing my belly. When I go swimming, I wear a pregnant bathing suit that I never made use of before, but now I quite like. It also covers all my stretch marks and doesn't hug my skin around my belly. All my clothes are like this.

Here I was, though, having to try on bridesmaid dresses and feeling very round and frustrated by dresses with slips that didn't fit around my waist—even when I went up several sizes and had my chest swimming in fabric. The hardest thing was having to imagine what size I would be five months from now, which meant for me—am I going to be pregnant or not? It was too much. But I wanted to think that maybe I would be, so I finally went with a dress that pinched under the chest and flowed out from there. I hope that I have either a six-pack or an obvious belly by the time that that dress arrives for the wedding.

A few weeks ago I went for a massage. Now I will only go to this woman that I have learned to trust with both my emotional and physical well-being. She is wonderful. She knows what I have been through and is just a ray of sunshine every time I go. At the end of one massage, she put one hand on my stomach and one hand on my heart. No one other than me had touched my stomach since the hospital. It caught me off guard, but then I had a sense that Little's T's memory was leaving my belly to go live in my heart instead.

It was a peaceful feeling, but one that also brought me to tears once the masseuse had left the room. Since then, I don't feel for Little T in my belly anymore. Up until that moment I hadn't liked people talking about Little T being in heaven. It's not that I had felt that he was still in my belly, but I had wanted him near to me. Heaven couldn't have him yet. Now I feel more at peace with the idea of him having a place in my heart and in our memories. Maybe it was a message too, that someone else would soon occupy my belly.

Reflections

Before returning to work, I felt the need to write and update people, as I would suddenly be around others again. I wanted to communicate in writing how I was doing, and how I was processing everything. This way they could read and receive an update from me, and not have to ask me in person how I was doing. I wanted to avoid those kinds of interactions. I also assumed that the following questions were the ones that were likely on people's minds. Was I ready? Had I processed my grief? Had I taken enough time to do so?

March 18, 2016

Blog Post; **"Ready to Give Again."**

I'm returning to work in less than two weeks. I am looking forward to it and I'm even excited. In the last few weeks, I have found myself wanting to connect with others, to listen to and care for them. My ability, passion, and compassion to hear what they are going through seem to be back. I take this as a good sign that I am ready for work again. I have been stopping by for visits at school over the past few months, and it has helped to make the return less scary. My colleagues have seen me doing well. I even gave a workshop which alleviates some of the stress over how I will be received once I return.

Yes, everything Daniel and I have gone through has been extremely painful. It's been devastating really, but we were not defeated by it. The things that were important to us before still are, and in some ways they are even more important now. Daniel loved literature and writing long before we ever had conversations about starting a family. He is currently pursuing his master's degree full time and has a part time writing job at Concordia University.

I love art, baking, music, fundraising for Malawi, organizing and coordinating, and caring for teens. I spent the last few months immersing myself in music, pottery, baking for Malawi, and helping with church organization. It wasn't about keeping myself busy and running away from the pain. It got me thinking about things other than just the painful memories—and it reminded me about who I am other than a mother. If that was all I saw myself as, or others saw me as, what reasons would I have to keep going? I had never even decided about having kids until two years before Little T. I enjoyed the freedom we had to pursue our passions and the time we had to care for others. I also thought, ever since I was a teen, that we would adopt if we ever wanted to have kids.

Recognizing that my identity is not only in being a mother has helped me a great deal. It's not a recommendation for anyone else, it's just been helpful in my experience. That being said, my being a mom is still a part of my identity. It's important that I acknowledge Little T. It's important that any other children that we may or may not have will know that they once had an older brother. We will never stop thinking about him. It remains painful and sad, but I won't shy away from it. It's what we must hold on to.

As I have gone through the experience of becoming a mom, I feel that I now have a new perspective on what a woman carries in terms of societal expectations. There has been a lot of talk lately about feminism, and if there are still things that women need to keep standing up for. I think there are. Society can often try to box in our identity and tell us who we are and (even more significantly) who we aren't. We should be mothers and we should be sure to squeeze it in by a certain age. We should give things up that we care about for the sake of our partners or families.

One woman might delight in being home as a mother and

another might not. I think the goal that we must still fight for is for society to stop having any opinions about the right or wrong way women should shape their lives—because each woman will experience everything differently.

Women who try to share their experience of what it's like to be a woman in writing, interviews, etc. are often criticized for trying to speak for all women, and for getting it wrong. You must realize that it is their unique experience alone. Why should they be trying to speak for all women, if they speak at all?

No man is ever scrutinized in this way. No one looks at their experiences and questions whether they are doing men justice by saying what they've said. They aren't encouraged to just stay quiet because they "aren't helping the cause." If you have lived in this life, you have a unique voice that deserves to be heard. Some might identify with you, some maybe not. Every voice has value!

The only thing I can do is to speak from the perspective of my own unique identity and experiences. Part of that is what happened this past year. It's important to mention that someone else might have experienced that year in a totally different way.

I can recognize what made me resilient through this experience and what helped prevent long term harm. The protective factors[9] that have been present for me have been too many to count. I recognize how fortunate I was to have had the grounding that prepared me in many ways to be able to face Little T's health concerns and then ultimately his death. To be able to face grief and not have defenses built

[9] In psychology and intervention, we talk of risk factors and protective factors. Risk factors are the things that make it harder for someone to deal with the difficulties that they face in life. Examples include poverty, lack of a support system or friends, traumatic childhood experiences such as abuse or neglect, and other major life stressors. Protective factors are the positive things in your life that help you move past difficulties.

up over time.

I experienced a loving childhood, with both parents giving us unconditional love. I had a happy adolescence. I have never experienced poverty or major illness. I was born in a rich country with all of my needs being met by health and educational services. My faith community has been sources of support. I know that I come from a place of privilege and that not everyone is as fortunate.

Daniel and I have had a wonderful love story (we have been together since we were seventeen and eighteen years old) and our love has only deepened throughout this life journey because we allowed each other what was needed without judging. We recognized the importance of joy even amid sadness, and we sought out the things and people that had usually brought us laughter. I was given five months off work but paid close to my full-time salary. This allowed me time to really process everything.

I have been allowed to deal with things in my own way, at my own pace, and without anyone having expectations of how this grief should go. No one has been expecting me to cry or not to cry at any given moment. No one has been expecting me to do specific things with my time off. No pressure has been exerted on me to return to work quickly or to take a longer time away as needed. I have felt no pressure to attend church or not. I also had many people watching me closely to make sure that I didn't slip into depression or severe anxiety. Protecting me from that, I believe, have been everyone's prayers and support. As well, mindfulness has been a good guide in allowing me to feel many different things at the same time, and to not judge myself for any of these thoughts or emotions. I have recognized that thoughts and emotions come and go; they don't define me or control me and so they need not be feared.

And so, with thankfulness, I feel ready and excited to go back to work, and to continue that chapter of my identity. There are so many teens who are growing up with numerous risk factors present in their lives. My passion in my work is to help tip the balance by being a supportive person in their lives and by listening to their unique experiences. I want to help them find their passions and I want to help foster a school environment that protects them. These hard life experiences don't have to defeat us. But we need each other and we need to respect each other's uniqueness in order to make this journey a success.

April 4, 2016

Journal Entry

I am back to work and have so little time to decompress. I feel that I have less time to allow myself to think of Little T. It's like I need to push it aside so that I can stay focused and on track. I miss him so much. A page has turned. It feels strange. I don't want to push him aside.

Reflections

My blog post below gives my readers a view of my innermost feelings and sadness, while remaining very focused on three things: the coping strategies that help me, my faith that grounds me, and my need to be alone with my grief at this time.

April 17, 2016

Blog Post; **"Soaking."**

At a certain point, people's support, listening ears, and kind gestures are no longer enough to help you cope with tragedy. You can't depend on these things to heal you or to make you forget your pain. They help pull you through rough times, but at some point, you need to learn to hold yourself up, and to stand on your own two feet—even if there's a bit of trembling at first.

Before realizing it myself, I started to feel the need to be alone—alone with my emotions and thoughts. It surprised me and scared me to think that I was changing as a person, pushing people away, and becoming a recluse. It has been happening on and off now since around the time of Lent, when I decided to make the focus of my Lenten reflection about feasting on water. I have continued to make it a priority to drink more water, take baths often, listen to waves or rain, and go swimming in the pool. I have also been looking up passages in the Bible about water and thinking about God's love washing over and calming my inner storm. After all, we're made up mostly of water, and as God's presence can be found in water, it must therefore be found in each of us.

In the new year I started going to the public pool. If the pool was too crowded, I would be distracted. I would try to swim at my own pace but then feel the pressure to swim faster or move out of someone else's way. I would often cut my swim short to make it to the showers on my own. In February, Daniel and I got away for a week to Florida. The resort we stayed at had a beautiful outdoor pool. In the evenings I would go for a swim and then soak in the hotel tub.

Not very many people were swimming on account of the chilly weather. I had the pool mostly to myself to spin, dive, float, and flip in. It rained one day and, submerged in the water with my eyes peeking just above the surface, I watched as the rain droplets ruffled the surface. I cried, taking comfort in being surrounded on every side by water. Pools and rainy days are perfect places for crying. No one can distinguish where the water droplets are coming from. You can be left to your tears without needing to explain them. After we came back home I continued my swims and my good deep cries. I left myself a lot of time to just be.

I have always loved water and being in it or in its presence. I love to listen to it, feel it, and know that it is life-giving and thirst quenching. I feel at peace in its presence. Now when I'm in the pool, in water, I am there to play, not to see how many laps I can do. I'm just being there and observing the beauty and tranquility of it. I feel myself move in it and the weightlessness of my buoyant body. I walk away feeling that I can face the day, or even the next few days before I need to return to it. Even drinking a cup of water or washing my face will draw me back to that feeling. When I drink enough of it, I feel refreshed. My body and soul have received all that they needed.

Perhaps the most powerful thing that this escaping to water has done, has been to allow me to take the time to care for me alone. These moments are not for anyone else. And yet, with time, I begin to feel re-energized and to think again about work and other responsibilities. I start to become eager to care for others. In the pool, other people no longer disturb me as much. I can set the pace I want and worry less about how this affects everyone else. I still haven't set any goals for myself, but I join the others in swimming laps. The tears still come but they are less invading and they come less often. My time in the pool serves as a good marker of my emotional state and my ability to be around and care for others.

I found a little fountain to put in my office and paintings of ocean waves for the office area. A motto of mine has become You can't stop the waves, but you can learn to surf. On returning to work, I felt that my cup was full again, and that I was now able to care for others once more. I told myself that if I became drained, I could just go back to the fountain, fill up, and be restored all over again.

Being back at work full-time has left me with less time to care for myself than I used to have. But I have been finding ways to do this during the day. I fill the fountain back up so that it can trickle throughout my day. I let a student wait a moment as I get a cup of tea and then settle back to listen to them. I take frequent washroom breaks (a trickling fountain in the background will have that effect). I find time for swimming once a week. I am learning now that my evenings and weekends must be more open to just me time—even if it's just for a ten-minute meditation. Other things that I do are listen to ocean waves, put on an album, or look up verses. I am allowing water to be the source of my energy and peace, and its outflow keeps me on a straight and trusted course.

The following are some songs, verses, and links that I have been meditating on.

"Song of Good Hope" (by Glen Hansard)

"River God" (by Nicole Nordeman)

Mindfulness-Leaves on a stream

https://youtu.be/r1C8hwj5LXw

"As the deer pants for streams of water, so my soul pants for you, my God."

Psalms 42:1 (New International Version)

"When you pass through the waters, I will be with you; and when you pass through the rivers, they will not sweep over you. When you walk through the fire, you will not be burned; the flames will not set you ablaze."

Isaiah 43:2 (New International Version)

"But whose delight is in the law of the Lord, and who meditates on his law day and night. That person is like a tree planted by streams of water, which yields its fruit in season, and whose leaf does not wither—whatever they do prospers."

Psalms 1:2-3 (New International Version)

April 26, 2016

Journal Entry

Mother's Day is coming up soon and I think it's affecting me more than I expected. I've been focusing on it so much because I'm reminded of the void that I cannot and will never fill. It's a role that I wish I could be celebrating right now, but instead I feel hollow—literally, as I remember how Little T used to be in my belly. I think of this more lately. I want to feel him again and talk to him again. I worry that if I ever become pregnant again, that once the baby starts moving I will freak out every time it stops.

Mother's Day makes me think of my own mom and my mother-in-law. I feel sad that I can't muster up the emotional strength to spend the day with them and celebrate with them. I want to say so much to them but feel that the only way will be to write to them.

Reflections

I am a mom, and I was with Little T, even after he had died. My mom was herself a mom, and she was looking at me as her child—her child who was suffering through motherhood's most devastating possible reality. My mother had two mothers, one adopted mother and her birth mother. As an adolescent I watched her find her birth mother and then deal with the complexities of both this discovery and the baggage that came from her relationship with her adopted mother. I watched this as a teenager and saw my mother experience emotional suffering. When I lost Little T, I witnessed others suffering as of a result of his death. It was hard to see my mom experience this suffering and her worry for me. In a way it made my pain multiply, as if I was feeling it through someone else's eyes— my mom's eyes especially. There is a beauty in the emotional partnerships that we have with mothers, sisters, daughters, and female friends—but right now I don't know how to deal with their empathy.

May 7, 2016

Email

Dear Mom,

I am sorry that I can't spend this day with you. I wish nothing more than to celebrate what a wonderful mother you have been to me but find this day simply too hard. I want to explain why I haven't been able to talk to you this past year. I worry that you think it's something you did or didn't do. Trust me— that is not the case. Your love for me throughout my entire life has made me strong enough to face this past year, and to keep facing it. Not for one moment in my entire life did I ever wonder if I was loved. You showed me love and how powerful it is. You taught me how to love others. The way you have led your life has taught me how to deal with difficulties and heartaches, and to seek creative and spiritual outlets.

You see, you did not need to say anything to me this past year; who you have been and continue to be inspires me. It helps to push me forward and to not get stuck in grief. You have overcome so much.

I don't know if I will ever be able to speak in person with you about Little T and everything that has happened, or about how I might be feeling at any given moment. I cannot face seeing your reaction to my pain. I know what it is to be a mother now and to worry for her child. How hard that is. I cannot see you facing that. It is too painful for me. It has a multiplying effect that runs too deep. It's not because I don't trust you or don't want to be close to you. It's just too much to bear.

I love you so much. Please never forget that.

Your daughter,

Elizabeth

May 9, 2016

Journal Entry

I understand now. I understand why people make decisions—bad decisions—that they later regret. I get how they can begin along a path toward self-destruction.

I really wanted to be someone else and to feel something else. I wanted to escape from my reality of being a mother without a child to care for. I didn't want to ignore the pain, but to pretend that there was no reason to feel pain. I wanted to live a different reality. I wanted one that was easier—a lighthearted one and one where I could imagine a different outcome. I only wondered and fantasized about it for a very short while, however. Because then reality hit. That life would be one without Daniel.

This has been a reality that we have shared. It is not just mine. What if our relationship had already had cracks though? What if splinters had already been forming before this tragedy struck? How much easier would it have been to not snap out of it and then to look for distraction? How much easier would it have been to look for something or someone else to take me away from my life? But it only took a few words from him to bring me back. I first had to speak of what was churning in me—this desire to be someone else and to escape. And then came his simple, honest response. "You can't leave, I need you."

Daniel's words brought me back. I realized that in the end we shared this pain, that we were facing it together, and that this was how we could help each other. We had promised to be strong for each other, to not fall into a depression, and to not give up. I couldn't abandon that promise and leave him. Suddenly, the fantasy wasn't so attractive anymore. There might still be great pain but there is also great love. I don't want to give up that love and so . . . I must learn to live with sadness.

May 10, 2016

Journal Entry

I have a new disdain for being a woman and for carrying the burden of bearing a child. I do not disdain the act itself, though. I didn't find pregnancy that hard, at least not when compared to the experiences of other women. Physically feeling the daily changes, pains, and discomfort wasn't the hard part. But now I remember all the waiting involved with pregnancy. I felt like I had no control and yet I monitored my body very closely at certain times each month. Was this the best time to try? Was this a sign of pregnancy? Then I faced disappointment month after month. Once I finally became pregnant, I started waiting for it to show. I waited for feelings and signs. But I was good about not being afraid and with going along with the pregnancy.

But now how will I be if it ever happens again?

Daniel doesn't have to go through this like I do. There might be this impression that it's hard for a guy, as he has no control over the situation and he just watches from the outside. But the illusion that a woman has control is even worse. It's the idea that it is our body and our decision—that it's that simple. Instead, I fret daily about what I could be doing to improve the chances of getting pregnant again. I want to initiate, but not program, our intimacy. I distract myself so I don't look for signs of pregnancy-- change in my breasts, tiredness or stomach upset. I feel guilty for having a few drinks. Maybe I am not ready for pregnancy again as I can't even seem to handle this part of it.

I am uncertain about my own body. I think of how it has forever changed but that there is no child to show because of it. So, I desperately want to lose the shape and the extra folds, but not the scars. They are mine to keep and to remember by. But the folds and the weight have no place. Or maybe they will eventually, so why bother trying to get rid of them?

I don't know what I want anymore. Do I want to wait or try again? Daniel says that whatever I want he is okay with. Again, it is my body, my decision. I will be the one stepping away from work and having my body taken over again. I can't see a positive outcome at the end of it, just like the first time we didn't have one. Is that what I fear? If I knew the joys, would I even let these other things overshadow it? After some sadness, and as another month begins, do we try again?

May 27, 2016

Journal Entry

I don't even know if I want a child anymore. Even saying that, I feel confused and guilty. I should have one right now. I am caught up thinking that we could have our lives changed forever by a baby in a mere nine months. It already has been. Except that we have the lifestyle of a young couple, with loads of freedom. I am enjoying having time for myself. Maybe it's simply because I need it. Having time to myself is healing. Maybe I still need more healing before I commit to everything that is required to take care of a child. Having Little T in my belly and having him present all the time seems more distant to me now. I didn't want to let him go for months. The wait before trying again was partly because being pregnant a second time would have felt like having him inside me once more.

Trying but not becoming pregnant was painful. Yet now I am confused about trying during the summer. I don't want the pressure of taking care of my body as if it is a vessel. I now feel so much guilt if I do absolutely anything. I feel guilty if I drink, have too much caffeine, don't exercise enough, keep too tense, forget my multivitamins . . . It all conspires to prevent my becoming pregnant again. Or even worse, if I happen to be pregnant already, it could cause harm. I am trying to figure it out, but it's hard and confusing.

Part of me wants to still try. I just don't want to have to wait more than nine months to hold a baby again. I think about what time of the year I would be delivering. Right now, it's looking more like March. I don't want my life to change for that to happen. Yet I don't know if I can really wait until after then. Waiting nine months to become pregnant felt like forever. Waiting eight months to deliver felt like forever. The last six months have gone by . . . it just seems a lot faster.

We have two weddings this summer for our closest friends; Sonia and Oli, and Maureen and Alim; and I am a bridesmaid for both. We also have the Osheaga concert weekend planned. At Osheaga alone I feel like I want to just let loose . . . with Daniel . . . and to have that time together. I don't want to worry about secondhand smoke . . . and I want to be able to have drinks.

This monthly cycle of grieving is rough. It feels very heavy; it might easily sweep over me. Am I deliberately pushing away thoughts during the rest of the month just to tell myself that I'm alright? Keeping up with everything else going on during the day causes it to all build up, until my body gives me the clear reminder that I am not pregnant and not with a baby. Suddenly it all comes crashing down, like waves onto jagged rocks.

I have tried to face this rather than run from it. I've tried to acknowledge when I am really feeling sad or fearful, but I cannot pretend that this happens automatically. It takes me a while to even realize what is going on.

I have an underlying urge to just look for a different reality, and to escape from what is difficult to go through, but I deny the urge and continue to sail on into uncharted seas.

May 29, 2016

Blog Post; **"Nowhere Close to Smooth Sailing."**

You might be wondering where I'm at as my blog posts have become less frequent. It is now harder to share what has been going on internally, and since there are no updates about Little T like there were before, I have less to post. So where am I at?

I am doing okay—more or less. Yet, when things around me change, or give the impression that they might change on me . . . the prospect that I might lose my footing scares the crap out of me. When something unexpected, unwanted, and tragic happens, you change your way of looking at things. You lose the sense that things will just work out in the end. You now know that that isn't always the case. Any changes that would not have even rocked your boat before, now feel like a tidal wave that will surely drown you.

I may not have been talking openly about my thoughts and grief to everyone around me, family included, but I have become dependent on your presence. You are silent witnesses to what I've been going through. My sister has been living with us for two years now, but this week she left for a three-month trip to Ecuador. It scares me to not have her close by anymore. I'm losing part of my support network. Someone's physical presence can be most comforting—you don't even have to exchange words. It's about having another person paddling in your boat when you get too tired to keep going.

My work family is another major source of strength for me. It's not because I pour out my emotions to them; there's no time for that during the workday. Besides, that's not the place for it. But knowing who they are, how they have cared for me over the past year, and the trust they continue to put in me gives me great strength. There have been a few times when I have needed to take a moment for myself, and they've given me the space and time without a second thought.

I recently learned that changes are coming this school year, including a big shift within the administrative team. This might sound silly to someone else, but the individuals who make up this team are the same ones who make up the supportive stronghold that I rely on at work. You learn to trust the people in your boat and how to paddle at the same pace. When that boat starts to rock, you can't help but feel less secure about the course being set, or in the stability of the boat itself— there's now some fear that it may tip.

My faith community also keeps me afloat and helps me to navigate the rocky waters of life. It's where I've learned to paddle, and to understand the waters we live in. We are undergoing some serious reflections about whether our church should continue as it is at all. There is discussion about what changes should be made and if we really have enough to keep it going. I realize that faith does not depend on the structure of a building, but having a place to go to, somewhere you know that you can go to be filled up and strengthened is important. It's the jetty we tie our boat to at the end of the voyage. It is a very rare thing in this world to have a like-minded body of people who are all striving to be their best loving selves and who are encouraging each other to do so. Facing the possibility of losing that place to dock at, to be redirected, feels scary.

And so, I can't help but feel a bit terrified. Waves of panic seem to creep up from out of the depths. I don't know how I will be in the months to come, but with many uncertainties ahead, the situation now feels much more daunting. I have been reminded about taking things one day at a time. I understand that all of my support systems consist of people—people that I can still find a way to talk to and relate to. And it doesn't always have to be in person. One of the most valuable things that I have been learning is to communicate clearly what I need. You, the people in my life, know how to respond and many of you have told me that it makes it easier for you to support me.

I don't have much control and I have great fears, but I take some comfort in knowing that the rough waters behind me have given me the strength to face anything that lies ahead—no matter how turbulent.

June 5, 2016

Journal Entry

"A baby is God's opinion that the world should go on."

—Carl Sandburg, Poet

What the fuck is this? So, what does that mean for Little T?! I hate these things!

June 6, 2016

Journal Entry

Is this feeling of panic, this overwhelming pressure bearing down on me, really rooted in my confusion about wanting to be pregnant again? There is all this work and church stress. Am I trying to hold things together while they fall apart within me? Am I trying to make sure things go well, even though it seems they are all fragmenting themselves? I don't know how best to capture everyone's voice.

We want things to continue to run smoothly, and yet at church, our Pastor, Nick, is pulled to other churches and can't even be there with us on Sundays to pull it all together. The boat is rocking.

At school, it's unclear who is even going to be left to run things. There are so many kids to think about and it seems that there will be no vice principal who even knows them anymore. I am trying to make sure that I have all their names and that their details are written down, so that they won't be forgotten. It feels overwhelming and endless—and perhaps a little futile.

It's like people want us to fail, and are going out of their way to make it happen. They want the church to fall apart, and they want the school to stop being effective at reaching out to students.

July 19, 2016

Journal Entry

I know I shouldn't feel this, but I am disappointed in myself. I am disappointed that I couldn't magically pull myself out of grief on my own. Apparently, I couldn't, and the pieces are now crumbling, or at least it's clear now that my sloppy pasting job is showing cracks.

The things I have been telling myself, in order to get through my challenging thoughts, memories, and triggers, have merely been feeding the beast of avoidance! This has caused me to detach from people so that I don't show my feelings in front of them. I always tend to hold back from people during difficult moments, and maybe that's no longer working. As a result, I've avoided letting anyone in. I have started to become a different person—someone I never wanted to be and tried so hard not to be. I need help to get through this—

professional help and lots of it. I suppose to be honest, I have for a while.

I already know a fair amount about psychological health, as that's a big part of my job. I have a lot of coping strategies that I employ to take care of myself, so I had figured that I would have been able to get through my grief on my own. But knowing what helps hasn't been enough. Now that I am off work for a few weeks, I realize that I still need time to heal, and this frustrates me.

What (I keep asking myself) is the problem?

When I am around others, I tell myself to be strong for them, to be there for them, and to not let my grief interfere with that effort. I do not want to see people in pain because of me. Right now I can write to people about how I feel, but I can't express it to them properly. I can barely sort out what is going on with me sometimes except that I feel overwhelmed.

Changes overwhelm me—more than they did before I lost Little T.

I am having trouble wrestling with the idea of becoming pregnant again, if, and when, it happens. I don't know how to navigate this; I feel lost in the fog. Maybe I still need healing before those emotions of going through another pregnancy and taking care of a child enter my life. At work I have had less time to think of Little T. I suppose I feel guilty for not thinking of him more.

I feel fragile and have trouble whenever I am not busy with things. I have talked with Daniel and a bit with my friend Kim, but it is not enough. Maybe I need meds, maybe not. I am open to the idea, as there are moments when I simply don't know if I can pull through.

Not taking care of myself before I try to take care of others is a barrier, and I don't know how to get around it. Maybe it would be a big help if I simply went to see someone who is solely devoted to taking care of "just me" for that hour. It would be someone whom I wouldn't feel any guilt about burdening, or about giving my pain to, and it would be someone to whom I would express everything in person.

I reached out to Louna earlier in June. She was my social worker from the Jewish, and we both agreed that I should see a psychiatrist at the Jewish. Luckily, the appointments aren't in the main Jewish Hospital but in a neighboring building. There would be too many memories linked to the hospital building itself. My first appointment is Thursday. I am seeing a PhD student, Dr. Kattan, from the Perinatal Mental Health Services Department.

Finally, it's my four-week summer break. I am no longer so busy and I can dedicate some time and headspace to beginning therapy.

Art is one way that I use to process some of my emotions and thoughts.

These ceramic pieces and paintings represent the dynamic going on in my processing of grief.

Walking with Grief, December 9, 2022 (oil on canvas). Photograph by
Alberto Porro.

Grief has often felt like a riptide. In the early years of my grief it would surprise and come at me suddenly and I feared it would pull be under and I would be powerless to resurface.

Riptide, Winter 2023 (oil and wax on canvas).
Photograph by Alberto Porro

This painting is based on a photograph taken in Iceland from our trip in 2016. The contrast of dark colours and lively greens came to represent the contrast and harmony of death and life that are both present. The loss experience and grief never quite end but life can still take form around it.

A space for death as well as new life, April 2023, (oil on canvas).
Photograph by Alberto Porro

November was always a hard month. I spent a lot of time on my own at the lake, sitting on the dock. On a misty or rainy November day, I felt like I was one with the backdrop of water and sky colliding in dark grey tones.

A November at the Lake House, October 2022, (oil on canvas). Photograph by Alberto Porro

The black silhouette represents the womb which is holding not only a child but the heritage of women that came before me and the women that will come after me of carrying the weight of pregnancy and loss. There is a family tree represented in the middle that acknowledges roots, connectedness, and a life that is growing. Each layer can be interpreted as a person currently or previously carrying a child. I also see it as the emotional history of my experience, with the haze of uncertainty (in purple), the hope and joy (in green and yellow), the anger which came later (in red), and the eventual acceptance and peace. The final layer (in blue), represents calm acceptance, and can be seen as water—surrounding it, carrying it, and keeping it altogether.

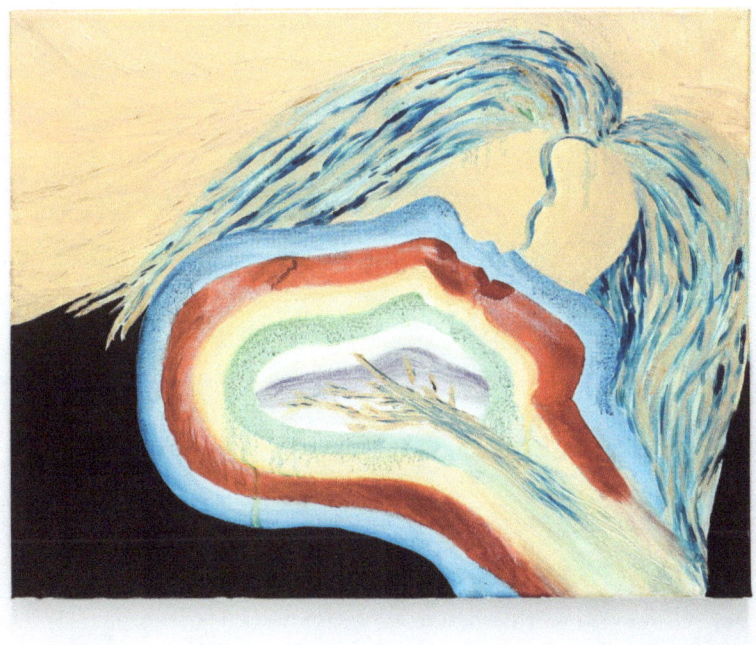

The various stages and faces of motherhood. February 2023 (oil on canvas). Photograph by Alberto Porro

Beauty in Shared Suffering April 2024, (Terracotta).

December 2022. In the pottery studio, trimming a ceramic piece at leather hard stage. Saint-Henri, Montreal.

Daniel and I in March 2015.

Laska, our husky, and me and Little T.

November 2016 Iceland Trip.

January 2018.

Finn and I having fun at 5.

And 6.

SECTION 3

Remembering and Trying to Forget

Between August 2016 and early May 2017, I received a diagnosis of post-traumatic stress disorder (PTSD). I met regularly for therapy appointments with a PhD student in psychiatry. As the school year resumed, I stretched out the appointments over two-week periods and took time away from work after appointments to process everything that we had worked on. Through this, I was making time to express to someone what I was and had been going through, and I was processing the start of another pregnancy. It was a period of reflection and of personal discovery.

August 20, 2016

Journal Entry

We went to the water park on our little vacation to Ottawa. One of the attractions was the wave pool. I really wanted to go in, but obviously I forgot how short I was and how much harder that would make it to stay above the crashing waves. Waves were charging in from two separate angles, one after the other. I kept thinking "I got this. Just count, and jump up and down real fast." Of course this didn't really work, and the waves kept crashing over my head. Daniel and

I both thought that this was funny until I would try to take a deep breath and end up choking on water from a wave that had just pounded over me. Daniel was watching me very carefully, and he often asked if I was alright. I was managing but it wasn't pleasant, and I was quite tired after the waves subsided. We went again, but this time I went a little deeper so that I couldn't touch the floor at any point. I now had to swim the whole time. I eventually got used to the motion of the waves and I rode them in one direction and then the other; I even spun myself in a circle. All the while I kept my head above water. This was an example of learning to adjust to a dynamic, changing situation. In a way, the wave pool was a fluid metaphor for what was happening in my life.

I went on my own to a lavender farm in the townships. I have recently begun to learn about the healing properties of essential oils, and lavender is one of the most popular as it is especially useful for calming. It seemed appropriate for me to take the long drive out after a meeting with the therapist and to go right to the source of this natural healing agent. The flowers weren't in full bloom at the time. I was a few weeks late for that but the plants, still a little purple, released their aroma when I brushed my fingers across them. I went alone but I wasn't lonely. It was just for me. I was tempted at the gift shop to buy lavender-infused beauty products for people that I knew, but then I told myself no. They weren't there and they might not appreciate it as much as me. So, I only bought it for myself.

I am glad for the new school semester and for being back at work. I am enjoying it, but I fear that I won't be able to manage taking care of myself while working, and that I will crash and need to go on sick leave. My psychiatrist is coaching me to not focus on whether that will happen, but is instead showing me that I am doing things to make sure that it won't, and that I need to just keep doing those things.

I am committed to appointments. I am even trying to take a full day off on those days if possible. She is helping me to take the time that I need to process things. She is reminding me that there is no one recipe for a person to follow in order to heal. She is helping me to remove the pressures that I manage to put on myself, like the pressure to be over this and the pressure of trying to manage other people's feelings above my own. But also, she is helping me to be kinder to myself, to gently face the things that I am avoiding, to ask myself why I am avoiding them, and to allow them to be painful, because they are.

Post-traumatic Stress Disorder. I can't even write it without wanting to erase its existence from the page.

I had to return to the Royal Vic hospital where I was supposed to deliver Little T. Appointments at this hospital to see the pediatric cardiologist were always the most painful ones. My therapist is helping me to create a list of things to gradually expose myself to as part of the process. The Royal Vic/Children's Hospital was way down that list. She would not have prescribed it this early in my exposure therapy, but my Uncle Wes was dying, and I wanted to be there to see him at the hospital and to be there for my dad.

Being there brought on flashbacks. I saw the uniform beds, the view out the windows, and the guest armchairs that are in every room. I saw my room. It had been the place that I had occupied when my pregnancy had reached thirty-five weeks and where they had told me that they wanted me to go home to take it easy and to keep Little T in my belly a little longer. I remember being so excited, and of having family around who were so hopeful and excited to welcome him into this world—to take on their roles as aunt, grandparents, and uncle.

I remember the large hallway, the way to the elevator to the pregnancy wing. That was where we had had the heart monitoring test, and where I had thought that I could still feel Little T kicking. But he wasn't. He was just floating in my belly. His tiny body was lifeless, a condition that I was completely unaware of until the doctor did the scan. We were so used to seeing scans and now there was nothing. His heart that had been moving, the one we had studied so intensely on so many hospital visits, was now forever still. I knew that it was coming, but the doctor saying the words, "I am so sorry," broke whatever last hope I might have still been carrying. I remember thinking that this was a movie moment. It was like I was witnessing us go through this the way onlookers watch a TV, and that it wasn't the actual reality of our lives.

Then Daniel took me in his arms, and I cried as reality set in. But first, there was a lot of anger. Just one week earlier I had been in the same hospital. I had been eager to give birth to Little T, whose heart rate had been just fine. That same doctor had been the one to tell me that I should go home to wait longer so that Little T would have a better chance. He would be stronger if we gave him more time in the womb is what she had said.

It all seems like a cruel joke now. It is so unfair. He may not have survived the childbirth or have taken his first breaths, but no one knows that for sure. Maybe oxygen machines could have kept his big heart pumping just long enough for his lungs to strengthen to the point where his body would have been able to face the many surgeries that they said he would need.

After he died, no one had talked to us about any of this or had explained the science of what had happened in the end. When Little T was stillborn, they had talked about the placenta being detached as the cause. Or had it really been that his heart had finally stopped after having to work so hard and then the placenta had detached? Or had it been something else entirely? I don't know why, but not knowing this still creeps up. He had been very sick, and the fact that he had lived for eight months had already been a miracle because of his various heart issues. But his dying had also been when the miracle had stopped.

Would all of this have been easier to bear if he had died at five months when we had first found out about his heart? I feel like we were being strung along by the ultrasound team, the cardiology team, and by God. The geneticist only kept meeting with us until she knew what chromosomes were affected. At that point she knew that there wasn't anything to be done that would change things. She never returned a call I made to her after he died. The geneticist never answered the questions that I had about the autopsy. Our case wasn't interesting anymore.

Louna, my social worker at the Jewish General Hospital, was the only one who talked about the possible reality of Little T dying before he actually passed away. In the fall before his passing, she was the only one who asked me to reflect and to voice why we had decided to go ahead with the pregnancy despite so many variables and the strong likelihood of him not surviving. She knew, from other parents I presume, that these doubts and questions creep back. Maybe answers wouldn't have changed anything, but Louna asking these questions to me allowed me to acknowledge the possibility of his death when I never might have otherwise..

September 1, 2016

Journal Entry

Realizing that it is September makes me sad. Just a year ago things were so different. I was at school trying to wrap things up, knowing that I would be off work soon and that I would have to start going to medical appointments once a week. A year can move so slowly and quickly at the same time.

An open letter to my new colleagues:

I wanted to take the time to let you know why there will be times when I am not at work. These will possibly be as much as once a week for part of, or perhaps even all day. I am excited to be working with you all and am very happy at work. But there are things in my life that still need some healing. I must make room for this, especially with the heavy type of work that we do with our students. Otherwise, things have a way of creeping up on me and I really don't want to get to a point where I can't be working anymore.

A year ago, at this time, I was six months pregnant. We had found out over the summer that the baby had some very serious heart issues, and the fall was filled with numerous medical follow ups. As of mid-October, I was off work. In early November, our baby passed away at eight months. I was off work for five months and came back late last March. The changes at work haven't been easy for me to adjust to, as the previous admin members had been so supportive and understanding. That being said, my worries about working with a new team were quickly dispelled, as you have all proven to be awesome to work with during the last few weeks.

Over the summer I was diagnosed with PTSD. I started weekly therapy and am really trying to take care of myself. Last week I thought it was okay to work from home after my appointment, but that did not prove to be a good idea. And so, I am going to block out the time that I need on those days. I will let you know when I am absent, and I thank you ahead of time for your patience if I can't get back to you that day.

Happy to be working with all,

Elizabeth

September 13, 2016

Blog Post

You should know that I have been given a diagnosis of PTSD and have been consulting weekly with a therapist. It has taken me time to accept this. My career has been spent taking care of others and trying to understand their suffering. I thought

I could understand my own and carry myself through it, but it turns out that I need outside support.

I am realizing that taking care of myself is not something that I know how to do. Nor do I express my emotions as well as I think I'm capable of. Underneath it all, I think that expressing anger and fear makes me a less joyful or hopeful person. My therapist is working with me to gently face the things that I have been avoiding. She is helping me to ask myself why the avoidance is there, and to allow situations to be painful, because they are. I am noticing that though extremely difficult, I can pass through these things once I face them.

Post-traumatic stress disorder is said to be a struggle between remembering and trying to forget. Memories are there and they do creep up—often unexpectedly. Because the memories hurt so much, I want to push them away, and not re-live the pain. I wish to forget so as not to have to go through the pain again, but it is impossible to avoid reminders.

There are many things that are still very difficult for me. For example, it is very hard for me to see, hear about, or be around babies and pregnant women. Certain hospital spaces we had previously visited for appointments bring back a lot of now very painful memories, even if at the time they themselves weren't painful. I am learning that I don't have to pretend that this isn't hard. It's okay. I need more time and I need to delicately face these things.

I need to be clear that I cannot and will not express these difficulties around others. Because of the point that I am at in my healing process, I will not and don't want attention drawn to the difficult moments that I may be going through. I need you to not change the way you would act around me in these situations. These are not moments that I want to share with others. That does not help me.

I am slowly accepting where I am now but there is still a long way to go. However, I have hope for where I might be later. I ask, though, that you be patient with me on my journey.

I take comfort in a friend of mine who ten years ago today, faced a tragic event in her own life and yet despite it, or maybe because of it, became the person that she is. Her experience marked her significantly, but it did not overcome her, or change her to the point of giving in to anger or despair. It should never have happened—and yet good still arose from a very horrible situation.

I am slowly finding some positivity again. I have hope, despite things still being stormy.

Reflections

Looking back on the summer and fall of 2016.

The struggle between remembering and trying to forget, with the ever-present reality of my PTSD, was all consuming. When I first started my therapy, I recounted to my therapist some scenarios of when I had been with other parents and how painful those times had been.

I wanted to forget my pain and Little T in those moments so I could carry on and not disrupt the conversations. A particularly harsh struggle occurred during my friend Sonia's bachelorette party. How oblivious I felt some of the bridesmaids were to my feelings. They mentioned their kids so casually; meanwhile, I was holding back tears and anger and trying to keep a polite face so that I wouldn't show my emotions. I did not want to draw any attention to myself or suddenly change the mood to pity or sadness for me. I didn't want there to be any awkward moments. I wanted Sonia to have amazing memories of her bachelorette and I did not want to pollute it with my pain.

When I discussed this event with my therapist, she allowed me to feel this deep frustration and anger. She really encouraged me to say no to future events (especially baby showers) that would just be too difficult to deal with.

Looking back now I know that I wanted to be a "bigger person." I wanted to persist and forget what I had been through for the sake of others. But I recognize, too, that remembering and feeling the anger was a necessary part of my grieving. It allowed me to feel—deeply—how wronged I was, when everyone else was allowed to have a normal child-rearing experience.

Dealing with my family was probably the hardest thing to go through. It wasn't because they were cold or unsupportive, but because they desperately wanted me to be open with them. They wanted me to be okay and they wanted to be able to do things to help me. They really couldn't though. Their grief was part of why I had trouble dealing with my own. I imagined how they worried for me—and how they had been robbed of becoming grandparents, aunts, or uncles.

The fall of 2016 was probably the hardest. The summer of celebrations was over. I was busy with work and the challenges with the new staff; I even took on more roles to help the transition go better. I liked being busy at work; it meant feeling something completely different than suffering.

The struggle of trying to forget was real. Yet I was so hard on myself for even wanting to forget the pain because that meant that I was trying to forget Little T. There was no way to forget what I had been through, both physically in my own body as it had changed, and in the world around me —because everyone I knew was aware of what I had been through.

I kept a sheet that I had filled out during my exposure therapy when my therapist had asked me to write down a list of traumas that triggered memories or sensations[10]. I needed to indicate whether or not I avoided these things and the level

---

[10] Form 6.4. Patient's Trauma Trigger Record from Treatment Plans and Interventions for Depression and Anxiety Disorders, Second Edition (Robert Leahy, Stephen Holland, and Lata McGinn, City, The Guilford Press, 2012).

of distress, on a scale of one to ten, that I felt when exposed to them.

The list included:

"Facebook pictures of people and their kids, especially babies." (4/10) *I unsubscribed from feeds of anyone I knew who posted pictures of their kids, and for some months I avoided Facebook altogether.*

"The subway or bus seat with the pregnant women sign." (2/10) *I would sit so that I couldn't see this seat.*

"Changing tables in public bathrooms." (2/10)

"Seeing little boys." (4/10)

"Seeing strollers, babies, and babies in carriers." (6/10) *I would look away or avoid being on the same side of the street.*

Then there were items that were not so easy to avoid:

"Bloating and my stomach gurgling." (4/10) *I would imagine for a moment that it was Little T kicking or moving.*

"Having a stomach." (2/10) *I didn't want to be mistaken for being pregnant when I wasn't anymore, and the fear of an interaction and the questions that this would lead to were anxiety provoking.*

The hardest things to face:

"Seeing my mom or dad interacting with kids." (8/10)

"People talking about grandkids, especially around my parents." (8/10)

"My mom." (9/10)

On the sheet I had indicated that this caused a lump in my throat, for me to hold back tears, and feelings of tension, guilt, and sadness.

FORM 6.4. Patient's Trauma Trigger Record

Patient's name: _____   Week: _____

Please list any sensations, places or situations that evoke traumatic memories, or that you avoid out of fear they might evoke memories. In the second column, write the memory or sensation that you get when you are in contact with the trigger. In the third column, note whether the trigger is something you avoid. Finally, note how much distress you feel (or would feel) when you encounter the trigger, from 0 (no distress) to 10 (maximum distress).

Trigger	Memory or sensation	Avoided? (Yes/No)	Distress (0–10)
seeing Sarah's baby	being pregnant together	Yes & No	9
bloating & stomach gurgling	Little T kicking	Yes	4
having a stomach	being mistaken for being pregnant when no longer	No	2
my Mom	memories - tense up, tight jaw that	Yes	9
the hospital - ultrasound clinic, Jewish	genetics, ultrasound clinic, waiting area, birthing room	Yes	4 3 7
the children's hospital	memory of labour, spa, present cardiology	Yes	5
metro seat in pregnancy sign	in the metro when pregnant on my way to appointments	Yes	2
changing pads in bathrooms	feeling of frustration & anger	Yes/No I look away	2
seeing strollers, babies in a carrier	feeling of frustration & anger	Yes I look away	6
pregnancy app → period predictor & daily notifies	feelings of guilt, frustration, sadness	Yes	3
talk about pregnancy and being a mother	tension, lump in my throat, avoid eye contact my	Yes	6
people talking about kids (especially around my parents)	sadness, guilt, lump in throat	Yes	8
seeing the word baby	frustration, tension, hold breath	Yes	2
seeing little boys	sadness	Yes & No	4
seeing my dad interacting with kids	sadness, lump in my throat, holding back tears, guilt	Yes	8
seeing my mom interacting with kids	sadness, lump in my throat, holding back tears, guilt	Yes	8
seeing baby clothes, toys	frustration, anger	Yes I look away	2
facebook pictures of people & their kids, especially babies	anger,	Yes	4

My parents were the most intense reminder of what I had been through and the child and grandchild whom we did not have. They would look at me with concern the way parents do. I avoided them because of this.

Moments with my mom and either seeing my parents around kids or hearing someone talking to them about their grandkids was brutal. It was the last thing on my list to eventually expose myself to. It was higher than going back to the hospital and higher than seeing babies. We never did "work through it" in our sessions by my being exposed to it. My therapist acknowledged that with PTSD some things are just never worked on. Not everything has a happy ending. They are accepted as just having to be that way now. Some things are just too hard to get past at certain times in our lives.

I was very short with my mom. I was mean, in fact, during this time. I wasn't done with processing other layers of my grief. Anger was surfacing during my therapy and in my own life.

My irritability and anger from when I was a teenager and onwards had always been directed at my mom. Ever since I was a teen I had had a hard time being nice to her. I had had the teen attitude of being annoyed at whatever she had said, even when she had had nothing to do with what was going on with me. Therefore, it made sense in some way that she would get the brunt of my anger now. She always seemed to take it, too.

I had so much trouble dealing with her worries for me. At the time of my PTSD, I didn't know how to deal with the empathy that she had for me. I really pushed away, which led my sister to be very concerned about our relationship. My sister wanted to fix this and so I widened my perimeter and started to exclude her as well—emotionally speaking. I couldn't fight it anymore as I didn't know how to look at their needs as secondary to mine. Whenever I was around my parents, I would just wear this brave face and it was really exhausting.

My therapist also asked me to fill out a PTSD checklist

questionnaire.

PTSD Checklist [11]

From 1 to 5, answer the following statements.

Repeated, disturbing memories, thoughts, or images of a stressful experience from the past.

I answered 4.

Feeling very upset when something reminds you of a stressful experience from the past.

I answered 4.

Feeling distant or cut off from people.

I answered 4.

Feeling irritable or having angry outbursts

I answered 3, although mainly for feeling irritable.

Avoid activities or situations because they remind you of a stressful experience from the past

I answered 3.

I can remember all of this. I still feel the same lump in my throat and the sadness. It does come back at times, but never as frequently as it did that summer and fall.

Trauma wants to be forgotten. It brings on pain, and we automatically want to block pain. When I blocked the pain of losing my child, I was also blocking Little T's memory, and memories were all I had of him. I would feel guilty for not honouring him. I wanted to hold on to his memory but so much of it was painful. I constantly wrestled with this dichotomy.

[11] Form 6.2. PTSD Checklist-Civilian Version (PCL-C) from Treatment Plans and Interventions for Depression and Anxiety Disorders, Second Edition (Robert Leahy, Stephen Holland, and Lata McGinn, City, The Guilford Press, 2012).

I look back now and realize that it wasn't just that I was experiencing irritability (described by so many grieving manuals as a "normal" reaction). It was also that I did not have the capacity to manage the many emotions in myself and in those around me. I had only enough energy to deal with the emotions that were surfacing from my own grief. Sorting through that was painful and confusing enough. The emotions of others just had to sit on the sidelines. My therapist repeated to me in every session that I first had to care for myself. My grief was heavy enough.

December 5, 2016

Blog Post; **"Ashes Where Hope Used to Be."**

You might be wondering, but 2016 has not been an easier year. In some ways I thought that it would be, as the constant worrying would be over. I thought that in some way we would have found peace, knowing that Little T did not have to suffer through any difficulties. But it hasn't been easier; it hasn't been any more peaceful. We don't get to see Little T grow up or get to see him face his significant milestones, even if they might have been different to other children's. Not being able to see him go through any is not better. Now, having passed the one-year mark, it is still not any easier.

Living in 2016 has left a ragged hole where hope used to be. I have struggled to connect back to my former positive self—a person who always wanted to look towards the positive and who had strong faith that going through difficult things would not be a reason to give up. I struggle not to judge that person now, as I feel that she was naive all along. Apparently, this is very common.

Envisioning a future of your child growing up and living a long life, and then to have this image shattered, leaves a deep mistrust of the future and a general distrust of anyone or of any beliefs that say that things will work out for the best. This is not a death where we can celebrate the person's life and remember how they impacted us and shaped this world for the better. It is a death and a grief process that is completely different. It is grieving only what might have been. There was no chance for Little T's life to significantly mark this world. He and we were robbed of that.

2016 has also been a year to question the place that church really has in my life. At the end of this year, the church that I have been attending for most of my life will close. It may merge with another church, but the way it exists right now will be gone.

I was not surprised by this decision. A small group of people can only share tasks for so long and a building can only stand if people have the time, money, and energy to care for it. Still . . . it is the gathering of people, people that I know and care for, that I will miss. They are people who hold on to a common hope but who do not claim to understand everything or to know all the truths . . . This had been a safe place to be for the last six and half years. It was a place where I had felt safer than I had felt anywhere before.

In 2009 our church had split and a small group had stayed on at St. Stephen's. I am not claiming that we were right or more correct than anyone else. In fact, that's the very reason why I stayed; I did not feel an urge to be a part of a meeting ground where everything was figured out and where the truth was so certain. That was not the path I needed. I also no longer felt the need to be part of a big community. I grew up in one, and it was easy at times to become lost in surface conversations instead of being deeply connected to fewer individuals. As I fell now into a smaller setting, I was able to become a part of some deeper, more intimate connections.

The split also led me to attach myself deeply to a homeless man by the name of Steve. He had been going to my church for as long as I can remember, but I don't think that I had ever spoken to him. Now, every week we would chat after lunch in the dining room. We were too small in numbers to meet in the big chapel building. Meeting in a house building behind the actual church made the environment seem cozier. It was once a shared student residence and so it had an actual bathroom with a tub. We were able to respond to a physical need of Steve's as every week he was able to bathe and put on a clean pair of socks. He was encouraged to share his insights during discussion time even though he had schizophrenia and was not always on topic; sometimes his insights were more "on topic" than those of anyone else.

I must admit, as new members joined, I was very hesitant to attach to them. I already had many friends in my life outside of church and I didn't feel the need to risk a relationship that might come to an end. Despite this, I have built new relationships and have grown attached to friends who have brought insights and encouragement that I wouldn't have found on my own. This is how I met Sarah and her husband Blair, friends whom I can be open and vulnerable with, and to whom I can express any emotions.

When we met together, we spoke about common beliefs but also about common questions. With them, there was always an underlying sense of hope that there was more going on in our lives than just breathing and living. There was a deep sense of purpose, drive, and even though I can't feel it much anymore, hope. When I did attend this year, I struggled with saying those words of common beliefs; I had many more burning questions than I had answers.

I could not confidently feel or express that same level of hope, but I liked being around it—as if over time it might resurface or maybe rub off on me. This was only possible because I trusted and cared for the people around me. I saw authenticity in everyone who attended.

For all these reasons, I will not be simply joining another church. I have no desire to be in a building of strangers and to go through the process of getting to know people all over again— people who I will not be able to make time for in my life. I have no energy to invest in sharing with others the difficult past that I have had. I have no desire to be a part of something that has a mission of seeking out more people and sharing with them this hope. I would be a hypocrite to speak of it. I have my own ashes of hope to worry about. I can only reach this level of trust with a select few people.

There is much recovery that needs to occur during this process. It is a process best done by gathering in a friend's home, with space to be vulnerable. It does not require me to plan or to give of myself to others or to be friendly with a stranger. My workday takes all that energy. If I carry any hope for change, the students I work with get it from me. I cannot give any more. My focus will now be on trying to find a spark in what feels like dry, cold ashes.

Meanwhile, I think about Steve. I worry for him as he needs a place to express his faith. He needs to feel cared for. He needs a bath, and he needs socks. He needs people to be kind to him and to ask him how he is doing.

Perhaps you can offer him a home on a Sunday morning or visit with him if you pass by his common stomping grounds every day. He is often panhandling in McGill station during the day and by around 4:00 p.m. he can be found in Central Station for several hours. He is usually at the McDonald's grabbing a tea and a muffin. He is perfectly harmless and perfectly kind. He has his little booklet of Our Daily Bread that he holds on to and he will probably quote you some Scripture. He has mastered what I can't: how to hold on to a hope that surpasses all understanding—even through homelessness and mental illness. Maybe he has rubbed off on me enough to provide a little spark. Time will tell.

Reflections

Looking back now I know that the loss of my church

community was difficult & left me without a space to anchor and talk about my faith.

It was also freeing as I was in a spiritual burnout. I had been trying for some time to make things work at church. I was plugging holes to keep the church afloat by doing secretarial work and coordinating Sunday services in a volunteer capacity. Again, for the benefit of others my energy was spent on upholding this church I had grown up in. My faith was itself unstable but having been in a role of service since I was a teenager formed a tendency in me to ignore my own need for replenishment.

When our church closed, it allowed me to look inward and be honest about things I was struggling with. Anger that been there since Little T's passing. Anger was never something encouraged in the church settings I was part of. Especially anger in women.

January 4, 2017

Journal Entry

I don't want to talk to people about Puffin growing inside me. I don't want them to hear my thoughts on these experiences, so I doubt I will be blogging about him now like I did with Little T. My emotions will stay mine, for now anyway.

I don't have any excitement about going through pregnancy again. My first is now just a painful memory of what led in the end to misguided hope. My body was physically reshaped and reformed and it never returned to its original state. It was a portrait really of my ability to hope.

This new pregnancy is, again, just something difficult for my body to go through. There will be unknown results at the end. What is the point of being attached? If in the end this pregnancy works out and a healthy baby is the result, then maybe I will attach. Maybe then I will think about what kind of a world I want my child to believe in and to be a part of. It will probably be a more hopeful one than what I see now.

I don't hold any guilt right now with the idea that my pregnancy will be one that I feel detached from. The baby inside will not know what I am emotionally going through. Nor should he or she. Let him or her grow in complete oblivion.

February 15, 2017

Journal Entry

Meg is coming home after being away for several months on her most recent trip to Ecuador. While she was away, she wrote me an email expressing how I have shut her and the family out and how I need to let them in and share my pain with them. I suppose that giving people more clarity, so that they know how best to deal with me, isn't a bad thing.

Here is my email response to her.

Dear Meg,

I have had trouble reflecting on how to respond to your email. With you coming back, I felt that it was important to find the words. I don't want to create distance from you and so to prevent that, I will try to express where I am at in response to some of the things that you wrote:

"You don't have to be strong for us. You don't have to pretend like everything is okay—and everything doesn't have to be okay."

I am not trying to be strong for anyone. I show my vulnerability when I need to—to Daniel and to my therapist. People mistakenly think that I am pretending to be strong a lot of the time. I am perfectly fine most of the time, but I am very aware that people are expecting me to be emotional or to break down at moments when they think I am affected, sad, etc. No one can either predict that or know what is going on with me, and I really don't like being analyzed at those potential moments.

I don't want to be strong for others, but I do protect myself by not showing my emotions to the family. This is not because I don't think you can handle it or don't want to, but because I cannot. The most difficult thing for me, more than my own grief, is to see my family concerned, upset, or worried for me because of anything regarding Little T. I acknowledge, more than you all think, how much pain you have from losing him and this is extremely painful for me. It is an empathy that has become unhealthy and too hard for me to bear. I have been trying to work on it, but it is extremely difficult. In other words, I take on others' pain, not just their grief—but their grief and concern for me. In the first months, that is mostly what I felt and there was a big delay in me processing my own grief because of it.

I cannot face that and so I push away if I feel that Little T will be brought up by any of you. This now extends to the new baby. I can feel some of my own excitement and also some of Daniel's, and I can mostly calm my fears of losing this baby like we lost Little T. I cannot fathom the thought of what would happen if something were to go wrong again, and of how it would affect you all. I couldn't bear to see you all in pain again. Therefore, it is very hard for me to hear of any of you being excited or of making plans for this new baby. I can't handle that.

You all have your own processes to go through and will do what you need to do. If excitement and planning is a part of it, that's fine. I just have trouble witnessing that. It just consumes me with a sense of dread.

"But shutting us out is only perpetuating the pain, and making us feel unwanted, unneeded, useless, and inadequate."

I am sorry you all feel this way, but I cannot fix that. Not now.

I don't want you to feel unwanted or inadequate, but it is not actually helpful for me right now to let you in on either my grief or my excitement for this new baby.

"In a way, it's kind of a joke to think that I've had hard times, too, because in comparison they're nothing. But sometimes it feels like I can't come anywhere near you, because I don't have a clue what it feels like to be in your position. I feel like my own pain is worthless and that it would be shameful to even mention it."

I am sorry you have felt this way, but I always want to hear about what is going on in your life, except for your grief over Little T or your concern for me regarding this. I haven't stopped caring about others and about what's happening to them. I haven't thought that what they are going through is any less than what I've gone through or am experiencing.

Your pain is your pain. It is your experience and it should not be looked at as any less. I went back to work and I have been able to care for and empathize with others without there being a barrier or judgment on my part. It would not be any less true for you.

"In one way or another, your pain is our pain."

It just can't be. This doesn't help me. And I know that you said that putting everything on Daniel is too much. Well, it isn't. At least he doesn't seem to think so.

"I feel like you try so hard to keep up this appearance of strength. I feel like you don't allow yourself to be vulnerable, and that you put up a protective wall. And I do believe that sometimes it's necessary in life to have that wall. But I think that in the long-term it hurts us more than it helps."

I don't know what the long-term effects are . . . all I know is what I can and cannot handle right now.

"Usually our feelings are worth discussing with the people concerned, no matter how awkward, uncomfortable, or risky

it is."

In some ways this is true but not right now, not about this. I am owning my own grief, fears, and emotions, and I am working towards healing. It is not anyone else's job to fix them for me. It is not for you or mom to feel that it is your job to do so or even to soften it for me. You can't.

"I want desperately to feel like I'm an important part of your life again."

You have never stopped being an important part of my life, and neither has Mom. I don't ever question how much you both love me, and my love for both of you isn't any less. My relationship with Mom has never been like the relationship that you have had with her. It doesn't need to be. I am okay with how things are, and Mom needs to accept that I don't need her as much as she wants me to. I will push back, though, when you try to mediate between us. It's not your job to do that. You need to let that be.

I will push away if you press on a topic that I don't want to get into.

I think Mom, you, and I spend a lot of time worrying about each other. Meanwhile, we are all very strong and we can seek help when we need it. We will find healthy ways to cope with our struggles. I don't need either of you to hear my inner ones. There are other ways that you can care for me and to me they are not any less important. They are what I need more.

Love, Liz

February 5, 2017

Journal Entry

I am four months now, but I don't really want to share the

news with people at large that I am pregnant because I don't want to have conversations about my pregnancy. My emotions are too mixed about it all, and I don't think that people can understand that. I don't think that they can understand where I am coming from. I myself feel some excitement. I also still feel sadness—it is all too familiar.

I haven't stopped thinking of Little T. I have many moments when I think of him.

Puffin's birthday will be in July. That is also the time of year when we had our first ultrasound with Little T. I have the ultrasound recorded. You can hear the doctor examining the different body parts. You can hear our voices of delight as we watch Little T's movements for the first time. Eventually there is a pause. The doctor examines and reexamines. It's the heart cavity. You can hear him say that something is wrong. There is silence . . .

I have started to feel the baby move and it brings me comfort. It makes me feel close to her. (The doctor said that the three-month ultrasound indicated that the baby was a girl.) I do feel some hope, and I am able to express this to Daniel. I can look at some of the baby things that we already have and start thinking about other things that I might want to buy. I don't want to include anyone but him in this. I don't want anyone else to be excited or to plan. I could only handle my own grief again, and no one else's. And no one should worry for me. Not until this baby comes and is visibly healthy will I consider accepting our extended family's excitement. I don't want any gifts. If they are excited and want to buy things, let them keep them in their own houses. I don't want to see them. I don't want a baby shower before the baby comes.

This is something that only Daniel and I can share together. It is our bond. It is something that we have started to build together and that no one else shares. She is already here. Her introduction to the rest of the world can wait. I only want Daniel's and my excitement during this time. We are starting to build our life with her—together.

March 8, 2017

Journal Entry

When the doctor had first told us that the baby was a girl, I had felt relief. I had told myself that it would have been hard if it had been a boy again. This way it would be less confusing. It would be easier to separate the identity of Little T from the new baby. Over time though, I started to feel sad that I wasn't going to be the mother of a boy and that I would have to wait until another pregnancy provided us with the opportunity to raise a boy. I was already a mother to a boy but I hadn't been able to express that or live it out. Strangely, this really affected me. I had had no preference for a boy or a girl before, and I certainly was against any gender stereotyping. And yet, I now wanted to raise a boy. This had once been taken away from me and now I was again sad with the knowledge that it wasn't a boy.

We had a more thorough ultrasound done. We told the technician that we wanted to know the gender and to our surprise she indicated that the baby was a boy. The biggest thing on my mind when we left the ultrasound was excitement. It was the excitement that I would have a baby boy and be able to raise him.

The baby had shown signs of perfect health, but the processing of that information hadn't been immediate. The visit to the hospital had felt more like a therapy session where I had been reliving a moment during my pregnancy with Little T. Or rather, it had felt more like I had been exposing myself to the environment in the ultrasound clinic to help reduce my PTSD. This would then have helped me to be ready for when I would (hopefully) be back when I was pregnant again. The appointment hadn't felt real; it had felt like it wasn't really happening.

Things only started to sink in later that day and that week. Some of the dread or worry began to lift. Everything had been normal. No doctor had been called in to double check the ultrasound in order to look at the baby's heart, or the surrounding fluid, or the ventricle spacing, or any other potential problem. Everything had been good and within the normal ranges. This had been what we had needed to hear. Now we could begin to hope again—we had facts instead of speculation. We had known how unlikely it was for something to be wrong with the baby again and that the pregnancy with Little T had been a fluke and yet . . . when you have been a statistic in the one in a million category . . . you don't think you are invincible to anything going wrong anymore.

The dread hasn't completely lifted; it comes back in moments or in waves but at least we have medical confirmation to hold up to the fears that creep in. I can hold them to the light of what we now know. The baby has no signs of developmental problems or delays.

Knowing all this hasn't changed much, though, in terms of being able to share my excitement with family in person. Daniel and I can hold onto hope and plan and be excited— but I still can't bear the thought of my parents or my sister making plans for when the baby will be here or asking me questions about the pregnancy and how I am doing. I don't want to hear from my mother-in-law about what she saw in a store or what she wanted to buy for the baby.

March 21, 2017

Journal Entry

Daniel and I are staying for a week with his parents while the bathroom in our apartment is being renovated. It is nice to have a bathtub that I can soak in at their house as ours has always been too small. I love having these moments to myself where I can be still in the water. My father-in-law is driving me up the wall as he regularly comments on how big I'm getting; he also asks if the baby is moving a lot. I haven't verbalized to him or to anyone that I don't want to discuss my pregnancy.

It is my body, though, and the new baby is in me. My stomach is not on display like an aquarium tank for everyone to peer into. No one else is allowed to build a relationship with him yet but me and Daniel. They can do that once he's here— not before. I know I can't prevent the family from becoming excited and hopeful on their own, but they need to do so in private and not with me.

Meg is still in Ecuador with her new boyfriend, Jorge. She sounds happy and I am happy for her. She won't be able to come for the arrival of the baby and that's okay.

April 4, 2017

Journal Entry

As I feared would happen if I was expecting another boy, I have started to feel very confused. I catch myself thinking about or talking to the baby by addressing him as Little T. Excitement is still an emotion that I am feeling, but what has become more present is sadness—again. This is not Little T. Little T is gone . . . forever.

To help me make a clearer distinction between Little T and the new baby boy, I started to look back on Little's T's ultrasound pictures to compare them to the new baby's pictures. How were they similar or different? It looked like their noses and mouths were different, but it wasn't enough to separate the two for me. To help me build an understanding of how they were different, without meaning to, I started focusing on what had been wrong with Little T, and what was healthy with the new baby. Little T had developmental issues and the new baby was "normal." I eventually caught myself thinking this way about my child, my Little T, and it brought me deep anguish. I fell back into deep grief and sadness. I was so upset with myself. How could I view my perfect child like that?

This has also brought on anger and a disconnect from the new baby inside me—as if he thinks he is better suddenly. I am angry at him now. People's excitement for the new baby also makes me angry. It isn't that I fear they are getting their hopes up again, only to be shattered. Now it's anger that they are not respecting Little T—his life, his legacy, his memory. It's that they are not grieving him still, but rather they are already celebrating the baby who is going to be here in his place. All this is happening inside of me. Only Daniel and my therapist . . . when I can vocalize it all . . . know how much in distress I am. Only they know how I am bitter towards the new baby. They know how I feel it is unfair that he will be physically surrounded by the love and support of so many when he is born. Little T never had that chance, and never will.

April 5, 2017

Journal Entry

I spoke to my therapist today. We discussed how my emotional processing is important but that it is materializing in an unexpected way. Instead of me feeling anger and then sadness . . . it has been the reverse. Sadness has been present on and off. Anger has been as well, but this is the first time that anger has been present when I have been thinking of the others around me. I am angry at them instead of being wrapped up in their emotions and concerns for me. Being angry at them has started a process: I am separating myself from them. I don't care what they are feeling towards me or the baby because it is incorrect. They don't respect me or my needs, and they don't respect Little T's memory. Of course they don't know any of this, and none of it is intentional on my part by any means, but it is how I feel.

I don't know how to process my feelings about the new baby. I am on Little T's side, not the new baby's, but I also know this is wrong, especially for a mother preparing for birth. How long am I going to hold on to this?

Tonight I opened a book again about grief after the loss of a baby.[12] I read about all the different emotions that one can experience, and how different circumstances can bring about different reactions in mothers. I read that the processing of this loss takes different amounts of time to play out for different people. There are no rules to any of it. Anger is a big part of the process and can come back again and again. Some mothers will never feel total resolution of their baby's death—that sense of loss will simply never go away.

I read how it is a common occurrence to feel a range of emotions when going through a new pregnancy, and that it is also common to memorialize the baby that died to the point of putting him or her on a pedestal that no other child could ever reach. It is common for mothers to hold in their memories the "perfect child"—the image of a child that will never be. The author discusses how this mysticism is in fact not the reality of any mother-child relationship. Babies and children are not in fact perfect and that holding them to that standard is not honouring them as that is not a normal parent-child experience.

Reading this last portion was probably what affected me the most. If I really wanted to honour Little T's memory, and to have an honest mother-son relationship with him, I needed to also accept his imperfections. I couldn't hold him to a standard that he would not have fulfilled in life. I recognized in myself that this was where I was. I was maybe even stuck there.

[12] Deborah L. Davis, PhD; Empty Cradle, Broken Heart: Surviving the Death of Your Baby; (Golden, Colorado: Fulcrum Publishing; 2016); pg66-pg88.

May 2, 2017

Journal Entry

I have now had my final appointment with my psychiatrist. I again brought up with her everything that I had been trying to process. The first thing she said to me was to give myself a break, and to not be so hard on myself for the grief, the romanticizing about Little T, the anger, and the disconnect towards the new baby. All was perfectly acceptable and allowed. It didn't make me any less of a loving mother. I needed to and could take the time to feel all of these things and not rush through them. None of them showed me to be an unloving mother but rather the opposite. I am a mother who is willing to be honest with herself, which will make me more aware of my emotions and better able to care for and honour my children. Even though this turmoil has been going on inside, I have not stopped caring for the current baby, keeping in good health during my pregnancy, eating what I know I should, and following up with doctor's appointments. I have even been buying and organizing items for the baby.

During the appointment I brought up that I have also been fearing that, when the new baby arrives, I will be caught up again by these emotions. I may be angry towards family when I see them caring for the new baby and forgetting about Little T. I may feel sadness that Little T will never get that physical expression of love through my touch and the touch of others. I worry that this may drag me down into depression; the new baby will need me but I won't be able to give him what he needs.

My therapist responded that she felt this was very unlikely. She didn't see that happening because, having worked with me for nine months, she now knew me. Of course I will have moments of grief and sadness, but she did not foresee me being consumed by them or being unable to function as a mother to the new baby. She said that all signs of PTSD were gone.

She told me to tell her how I had changed and what I had learned through the therapy. We discussed how I had allowed myself to take the time to feel and to express my emotions. We considered that the fear that they would overpower or overwhelm me was almost completely gone. Taking the time to care for myself when I needed it was now integrated into my personality. I was no longer exclusively thinking of others before myself. We talked about how all of these things will be lifelong lessons to hold onto. They will make me, in fact, a better mother to my children and better able to care for those around me. As well, I am now able to vocalize in writing to those around me what I need, and this has been helpful to me and to them. It is something that will continue to strengthen my sense of being understood by others.

Reflections

My therapy appointments with Dr. Kattan were ending because she was moving back to her native country in a few weeks' time. She reflected to me how far I had come in my journey through PTSD and she felt that it was a good time to end the sessions. She said that, while the painful moments and memories were still there, they now belonged to a normal grief experience and were less associated with PTSD.

In the following two months, before I gave birth to Puffin, I would continue to have flashbacks of trauma moments, and I would still experience triggers. However, they didn't send me into the same downward spiral that they would have before.

During our earlier therapy sessions, I had been struggling with having hope for the future and whether or not I would ever be ready for another pregnancy. During the first stages of my pregnancy with Puffin, I had not been able to hope for his safe delivery. Now my ability to hope that I would deliver him safely was growing by the day. Continuing with Dr. Kattan would have been helpful leading up to the birth of our second child and afterwards because anxiety was very much still present. However, she expressed a confidence in my ability to allow my feelings to be present, she reminded me to not judge my emotions and thoughts, and she encouraged me to rely on the tools that I had already been using to take time and to care for myself. I wasn't stuck anymore.

SECTION 4

Love and the Integration of Sadness

Exactly one year after Little T's passing, in November 2016, Daniel and I took a trip to Iceland. It is where we had hoped to go on our honeymoon back in 2010, but, because of the volcanic eruption at the time, the trip had been cancelled. We had gone to the Yukon instead and that had also been beautiful. Going to Iceland was a trip that we had long since postponed, but it was exactly what we needed. We were away together, just the two of us, in a space of natural beauty. I was in awe. I was faced with the sublime all day long as I looked with fascination at water in all its complex states. We would be driving and on the same day see waterfalls, ocean waves, geysers, caverns, and then sheets and blocks of ice.

I now look back on the natural beauty and I see a strange collision of dark black lavalike soil and lush, bright green life and colours.

I reflect on what had happened on this trip—unbeknownst to both of us. We were mourning Little T, and, Little Finn (Puffin became his nickname in the womb) was conceived. Life was taking form in me. It was a place—a meeting point of our lives together as a family. When we returned home it was a few weeks before I knew I was even pregnant.

Between May 2017 and February 2023, I continued to journal.

I also shared a couple of blog posts to introduce people to Finn, our second son. During this time, Daniel and I finally got a chance to parent. I was also processing the sadness that resurfaced from the loss of Little T, and I had some anxiety in myself that needed tending to. Being around family was a lighter experience now. My journaling, beginning therapy once again (now with a psychologist), and continuing to express myself with art, would all help to fuel my reflections. They would awaken a sense of the mark that Little T was able to make on this world.

May 24, 2017

Journal Entry

I am now over seven months pregnant, and exactly two months away from my due date. I feel that the whole pregnancy process is way too long. Those two months feel like forever, and I have a feeling, unexplainable really, that I will deliver before then, and maybe even well before then. I think this is partly because, as of a few weeks ago at least, everything in the pregnancy literature regarding births in Western nations indicates that the survival rate of a baby born at this point in a pregnancy is very high. Since this little baby inside me shows all the signs of being healthy and developing normally, he could be born today and be totally fine. Maybe he would have a longer hospital stay, but he would be fine. I wouldn't be worried, and I would get to hold him sooner. I would get to see him, touch him, and see him squirm and move. And Daniel would too. I don't want to wait for any of this, even if it meant that he would be at a better birth weight and could regulate his own temperature if he was born later. I want to see him now.

I think behind this is also a fear as I approach the thirty-five-week mark. That was when I went into preterm delivery with Little T when he was still active and moving. He still had a heartbeat that we could hear and see on the monitor.

I was sent home though, and less than one week later it had happened—his heart had stopped beating and his breath had stopped, to never begin again. I hadn't even known that it had happened. I didn't get to see him or hold him when he was alive. I still have anger and sadness that I might have had that chance, but it had been taken away.

I know that logically it doesn't make any sense. By trying to get further in the pregnancy I was ensuring a better chance of his survival. Had he been born at thirty-five weeks he might not have survived and he may have even experienced pain or distress. He might have been rushed to surgery or to a breathing machine and I wouldn't have been able to hold him anyways. Maybe in the birth itself he would have died. But . . . yet . . . I still wish I had delivered that day.

I am still worried that this will happen again somehow. I don't trust the process of pregnancy. I want to interrupt it myself. Allowing nature to take its course did not work for me before.

I have been to the hospital twice in the last month to make sure that everything is okay. Once I had false contractions, and the other time I had terrible heartburn and a persistent cough that was keeping me up at night. I was not worried about the baby or my pregnancy. I had just wanted to be sure that I was not dilated too much and on the second trip I had also wanted to double-check my breathing as my chest was feeling tighter and more constricted. At the back of my mind, though, I had secretly hoped that the birthing process had in fact started.

The visit to the case room to monitor my contractions was especially comforting. It wasn't because I showed no signs of being dilated or that the contractions had subsided, but rather that I was in a hospital bed and connected to a monitor that showed Puffin's heart rate. Daniel could also hear whenever the baby moved because the heart monitor made a steady and audible sound. He was really able to share in the experience of knowing that our baby was moving. The baby was there. He was alive and well. We also got to see another ultrasound of the baby moving.

On the second visit, it was comforting to see an ultrasound again and to get some reassurance that pills would help to relieve the heartburn in a day or so.

I don't think I am being irrational in trying to move the pregnancy along faster. I don't think I am taking or will take unnecessary trips to the hospital, but I do still hope for an earlier delivery. I am thirty-one weeks now. I don't know how I will emotionally and physically react to hitting the thirty-five week mark and then the thirty-six-week mark. Stress can also bring on contractions. I am keeping my mind busy with work, but that might be both good and bad.

My body is preparing for breastfeeding. I am beginning to lactate. Annoying as this is, again I wonder if this is a sign that I don't have too much longer to go. Lactation brings about difficult emotions as well. Right after delivering Little T and leaving the hospital, I began to lactate. I was at home for several weeks processing grief while I dealt with lactating breasts—breasts that had no use.

The smell of breast milk now brings memories of those early days. They are memories of intense grief, physical pain, discomfort, and the harsh reality that I did not have a baby to care for, despite having carried him for eight months and having given birth. I wonder if I will be caught off guard with this again when Puffin comes into this world, or if I will have trouble breastfeeding as a result of the negative association that I have of breast pads and the smell.

September 20, 2017

Journal Entry

It's no wonder that I have had no energy to journal about

Finnegan's arrival and thereafter. My hands are always occupied. When they're not, I use that time to quickly eat or shower.

On July 4, after twenty hours of labour, Finnegan was born. Although the delivery was long, it had not been that painful. My doctor, knowing about my previous experience with Little T, had said that there was no reason for me to experience pain during this delivery. Even up to the final minutes before Finn's arrival, my breathing had been controlled and calm, and the pain had been manageable. When Finn was finally born, I had my eyes shut. When I gave birth to Little T, my eyes had been shut as well, as I had wanted to wait to see him wrapped in a blanket; I had not wanted to see any defects. After Finn was born, I didn't open my eyes until the doctor told me to. He let me know that I could look at my son, alive and well.

Finn arrived three weeks early and in perfect health. Breastfeeding went very well. It was instantaneous as I held him for the first time; he had immediately made an upwards climbing motion towards me to start nursing. I was relieved that he took to breastfeeding so easily as I knew that that is often not the case. Maybe this was a way to help us connect. Since then, he has never wanted to stop.

Finn has reflux, and he can't lie horizontally on his own without throwing up and crying a lot. What has worked for us instead, is for him to sleep on me. My days and nights just blend. We spend a lot of time on the couch, dozing off and on. Daniel and the family all take moments to hold him and rock him. He is rarely left lying on his own. I know that I need him close. It leaves less time in between for fears or worries to creep in. It gives me peace and Finn is more peaceful that way, too.

Reflections

Looking back on the first six months with Finn.

We mostly spent our days and nights sleeping, cuddling, and feeding, but Finn's personality would surface at key moments. I have videos of him in the bath; he is looking ever so curiously at the water. He isn't fearful of it, but, in my eyes, his curiosity is obvious. When we took walks, he would always be looking out and around. On Daniel's birthday in September he cracked his first smile. At three months old, when he was left unstrapped for a few moments in his car seat in the house, he quickly wiggled down and out of it. He was always on the move. He held himself up and pulled himself along the sofa benches in the living room to reach a toy or to get back to Daniel and me. My parents and Daniel's parents were a constant presence, and everyone loved to hold him. In awe I watched them look at Finn; I felt joy—uncomplicated and peaceful joy.

January 23, 2018

Journal Entry

Poor Finn has his first cold, with a stuffy nose and a wet cough; to top it off he has teething pain, too. Nights are bad and just now he has refused feeding even though he needs to keep hydrated. Internally, I worry. I think every mom worries, especially the first time their baby gets a bad cold, but my worry feels a lot deeper. I worry about seeing him sick and that it will get worse. I worry that he will never get better. It's not a logical worry. There are no signs that my perfectly healthy baby will get taken over by a common cold. Yet it's a deeper worry, nevertheless. It's the worry of a mother who also grieves the loss of her child. A worry that is grounded in the reality that life is fragile and even transient. It's the realization that all children are not always protected from illness or disease or fluke genetic mishaps.

I don't often worry for Finn and his health. His medical visits have always shown what a healthy, happy boy he is and that he is completely on track in his development. Daniel and I hold on to this and live by it with confidence. It's bigger than just confidence. It's a choice that we have made to celebrate every day. We celebrate every day with Finn and we don't allow fear or worry to cloud our time or interactions with him. We want to raise our son to show him that every day has joy in it. We don't want to hold him back from discovering things or from laughing all the time. We are aware that he is watching our reactions. He is looking at us to learn how to read every situation and to gauge how to approach it himself.

My anxieties and fears are my own and I work on them internally. Right now, I am writing because writing helps to soothe worry and to calm those ruffled waters of concern that I always have in the back of my mind. It helps to get it out and to not keep it trapped inside. Writing allows me to express my fears without letting them consume me. They are out on paper now. They don't have the same hold. Writing also allows me some reflection. It is a chance to re-think something that I thought was certain. It seems silly now how I took cold symptoms to be so dangerous and something to lose sleep over when sleep is such a hard-won commodity right now. And yet, I give myself some slack as I am just a mother who loves her son and who doesn't like to see him in any distress. I am also lacking sleep.

Finn won't see any of this worry in my face. He may get extra cuddles, though.

February 20, 2018

Blog Post

I haven't written publicly in a very long time, but I have kept journaling. It may seem strange to you that I am now picking up where I left off in December 2016, considering all the time that has passed. However, I didn't want to write publicly in 2017 as I was pregnant again and I was going through many emotions. I was reliving the trauma from my first pregnancy and I had other concerns as well.

Since then, we have welcomed our second son, Finnegan Daniel Bartlett. The sharing of these posts in the past helped me to process and to communicate things that I had had trouble saying in person but that I had needed to get out. I now want you to know what is going on in our lives and I want you to hear about Finn.

Finn was born on July 4 in the early hours of the morning. I was thirty-seven weeks pregnant. As I had guessed would happen, he came early. The second pregnancy was not something that I had wanted to share with anyone publicly. I had had a hard enough time allowing even family to share in the experience. I was just too fragile. I was seeing a therapist and journaling then as well. Grief was ever present during the whole pregnancy, but then again, how could it not have been?

February 21, 2018

Blog Post

Finn is now six months old, and we are having so much fun watching him grow, laugh, roll, get teeth, start solids, crawl, and stand. As so often happens with parents, we were asked within days of Finnegan's arrival when the next one would be coming.

Will Finnegan have siblings?

Discussions about having more children and the order of siblings ("first born," "second born," and so on), are extremely painful things for me to hear. Little T is our firstborn child. He is our first son. He is Finnegan's older brother. Finnegan is not the "first," or "only child," or "only boy". He already has a sibling—a brother. He never will get the chance to meet him, but we will not deprive ourselves or Finnegan of Little T's memory, or of the reality that he will always be a part of our family.

The result of Daniel and my current discussions about having any subsequent children (the terminology we prefer) is that we don't plan to. So many difficult emotions were present during both pregnancies. Physically, the pregnancies also took a toll. Being deprived of raising our firstborn really made us want to focus on and celebrate even more all the little moments with our second. We want to watch every part of Finn's growing up with awe and joy. We don't want to miss a moment of it. We want to do right by him.

It is a natural thing to ask this of someone when you see them with a baby. "Is this your 'first'?" Up until now, when we have been asked this about Finn by someone who we don't really know, and who will also likely remain an acquaintance, I, and as far as I have observed, our family members, have all simply answered yes. Every time this has deeply hurt me inside. But then again, the idea of opening the deepest wounds in my life to a stranger is less than appealing. The simpler yet false response is painful but probably the better option under these circumstances.

With friends and family though, I want Little T to be acknowledged. You know our story and so I ask you to acknowledge it. Acknowledge our first son, our firstborn, Theodore "Little T" Bartlett. He is a part of us and will be a part of Finnegan's story.

Little T is short for Little T-Rex. It was a nickname that we gave him when I was pregnant. It really caught on—so much so that we received gifts for him in the T-Rex and dinosaur themes. I've held on to these and Finn has been wearing these clothes as he grows into them. When I get him dressed, I tell him that these were his brother's clothes. They are Little T's hand me downs.

Just recently, Finn started to play with a plush T-Rex that was given to us when I had been pregnant with Little T. When I took it out to show Finn, he instantly smiled and got excited. Seeing him hug it or grab it makes me so happy. It also makes me sad. I have spent some time worrying about what it will do to Finnegan to have parents who grieved, and continue to grieve the loss of their firstborn. How strange it will be for him to be the first visible child of the family and the "only child" but not actually the first one. Acknowledging Little T may bring about some strange psychological effects. However, hiding from Finn the reality of his brother by telling others to never bring it up and by never talking about Little T ourselves would be more damaging. It would also not honour Little T's memory or our emotions. It may be sad at times, complicated, and even strange for Finnegan, but I have learned to not fear complicated or mixed emotions but rather to embrace them. We will teach Finn to do the same.

July 4, 2018

Journal Entry

Finn is now a year old. It's quite incredible that a year has already passed. Although he keeps me busy and sleepless, time moves both quickly and slowly. He started walking in May at the age of ten months. He continues to thrive by being on the move. He is so smiley and joyful, and he loves being around everyone all the time. We are currently staying with Daniel's parents, Debbie and Kenny. We have packed up our whole apartment and we will eventually be moving into a construction site as our new apartment is being renovated. It is good that Finn loves to be around others, as after our apartment is finished, the renovations to my parents' apartments above us will take place, and then above that, Meaghan and her fiancé, Jorge, will have an apartment. Once everything is completed, Finn will be exposed to his extended family all the time.

July 23, 2018

Journal Entry

I have been thinking a lot about friendships and the people who helped carry us through our most difficult times. Seeing people was a very significant part of why Daniel and I pulled through our darkest hours. Really, I guess it allowed those times to not be so dark after all.

It was not the giving of advice or of lots of hugs or the crying with us. Our friends followed our lead in what we did or did not want to discuss. This usually meant not talking about any of it, but instead just being together—as we usually were. We hosted lip sync battles where we all brought our "A-Game." We performed carefully prepared songs and laughed with each other. We had a scheduled TV night on Wednesdays and faithful friends showed up every week. It didn't need to be said that we needed this or that we needed them. They just knew that this was how they could care for us.

In the first months after Little T's passing, we received food for our freezer which had lovingly been prepared by friends. That first year was filled with Christmas gifts, New Year's celebrations, wedding showers, bachelor and bachelorette parties, and two beautiful weddings where we danced the night away. That summer I was in the bridal parties of two of our closest friends. It was also when I was really starting to suffer, when I began therapy, and when I was eventually diagnosed with PTSD. However, I did not let myself be pulled under (as I had during the first couple of months) to the point of not celebrating with friends. I simply no longer wanted to be robbed of all the joy and celebrations in life.

Truly I had a wonderful time and I made memories for a lifetime. Even though I was in perhaps my darkest mental state, there was still room for joy and laughter and music and dancing. I was allowed to be more than just someone who was suffering or in mourning. None of my friends were checking in on me with an "Are you okay?" in those moments of celebration because, truthfully, I didn't want or need that. I really was good—in THOSE moments.

And in my solitary moments . . . well . . . I wasn't, but it wasn't up to them to fix that. Therapy was my space for that.

September 14, 2018

Journal Entry

I am sitting at the cottage and looking out at the lake. I see my dad, Mom, and Finn, who is now fourteen months old, set sail in the kayak together. It's a beautiful moment that I am trying to capture with a photo. I am both delighted and stirred by the emotions of what has transpired in the past two years.

At times during that first year after Little T's passing, I would watch my parents and think how blessed our children would be to have them as grandparents. It brought me such sadness at the time because I couldn't express this to anyone. I could picture moments like the one today and feel such heaviness. I couldn't give this simple pleasure to them. Little T, even with his heart issues and any other medical issues that might have appeared, would have been surrounded by care and by love. We had all been getting ready to care for him. And then . . . he was gone! He left a huge vacant space that none could really fill.

Two years ago, I did not want to do things as a family. I didn't want to go for little kayak rides or have gatherings of family and friends with kids running around. I chose to be in a kayak on the water all alone so that I could be with my thoughts and emotions. There was so much to process, and I had no energy with which to build new memories with my family. Memories of what "should have been" were taking up all the space.

No one could have rushed me through this and taken me

to where I am now—I was a more withdrawn person at the time. But I am learning that I sometimes needed to be alone to get through it all, that my deliberate solitude was part of the healing process. I had to do it by myself, and with the help of others, as difficult as it may have been to see me like that. I may be different now, but I was who I needed to be at that time.

October 15, 2018

Speech Excerpt

Shared at the Pregnancy and Infant Loss Awareness Day event at the Jewish General Hospital.

It is important to talk about perinatal loss and have an awareness day. It is such a deeply life altering event to have occurred to someone, and to their family. When we try to gloss over it, or treat it as a small grief that will go away in time, or that will be rectified simply when another child is born, we are dismissing a huge part of that person's and family's life experience.

We are not acknowledging the individuality of the child and of future children—now lost for all time.

When we are expecting a baby, we have experienced months of anticipation and physical changes to our bodies. When we have allowed ourselves to hope and plan and dream for the life of our child (and have maybe even seen the baby move in an ultrasound) and then that baby dies in the womb or shortly after, that baby does not just vanish. Even if the child did not grow up in this world, he or she will always be our child. The baby is etched into our personal life story.

I acknowledge how deep my experience was. Having gone through the trauma of perinatal loss, I am very attuned to the reality of a hospital that has now become a traumatic place to re-visit. But I also returned to the Jewish General

Hospital for my therapy sessions and was guided, as part of exposure therapy, through the halls of the delivery area. The hospital was no longer just a place of trauma but also a place of healing, a place of renewed hope.

I want to deeply thank the Jewish General for taking the time to annually acknowledge perinatal loss and to have put it in a memorial; a Magnolia tree was planted so we have somewhere we can go. Some of us may not have a burial site to visit. This space allows us to experience a connection with our baby. It is a further demonstration of how deeply the Jewish General team cares. I felt during my whole experience that Louna and the team supported me, cared for me, and were sensitive to my family's needs.

Having you here today speaks wonders of your strength, as walking even near this building must stir up a world of emotions and memories for many.

What must also be acknowledged today, is the strength that you all have as mothers who have experienced perinatal loss, and the dedication of the families who supported you through it all. Being a mother, father, grandparent, aunt, or uncle who is willing to be honest with him or herself will in turn make you more aware of your emotions and will make you better able to care for and honour the children in your family. Continuing to acknowledge our loss and to talk about our children is hard but it is important. Our baby also brought us a lot of joy, which is why the pain is felt so deeply. We must also remember that joy.

Reflections on October 15, 2018

October 15 has been a complex day for me—but in 2018 it had an added layer of complexity. Meg was in Ecuador getting married to her fiancé, Jorge. My dad was there with them and meanwhile, Mom, Finn, Daniel, and I were at the Jewish General Hospital for a memorial service for Little T and the many other infants that had been lost. I spoke at the event and then quickly pivoted to go back to my mom's house to join in a live Zoom virtual recording (set up by my dad) of the wedding judicial ceremony. My mom and I got ready by listening to catchy wedding tunes and we danced around with Finn as if we were heading to the actual event. We were teary-eyed as we watched the wedding. Jorge's family and Devon joined us on the Zoom chat which really showed how much our family was growing.

My mom is amazing. She was present for both her daughters through the many emotions we felt that day. There was no less sadness and no less joy expressed for either one of us. She expressed tears of sorrow as she carried the heavy weight of sadness for Little T and then later that same day she expressed deep tears of joy for Meg.

In October, Finn, Daniel, and I waited for renovations to be finished on a five-plex that my parents had bought in Verdun. The ground floor was going to be ours, my parents were moving into the second-floor apartment, and Meg and eventually Jorge were to move into one of the third-floor apartments. We were in the old, smoky walled third floor apartment at the time. I was often at home with Finn to weigh in on renovation decisions for our floor.

I travelled with my parents and Finn a couple of times in the years 2017–2018. My dad was attending city manager conferences across the United States as the president of the International City Managers Association. I saw a lot of my parents; the distance that used to be there and the wall that I had put up to protect myself were never really discussed. They just seemed delighted that I was willing to slowly take it down. This was so much so that I (and Daniel) were willing to live right below them. While our relationship is far from perfect, I have gratitude that it survived despite the trauma of us all losing Little T. Time, my work in therapy and Finn's arrival seemed to be enough to heal in me the PTSD symptoms that had related to my parents.

February 20, 2019

Journal Entry

I have felt things very deeply again—things that I thought I had emotionally forgotten about.

Sarah just had a health scare with her six year old daughter. She had been having eye issues and my friend took her to see an optometrist. That same day she was referred to the emergency room for scans and the next day flown to the BC Children's Hospital in Vancouver to have more tests done. Two days later she had an eight-hour surgery to remove a brain tumour. I wanted to do something to support my friend but here I was at the other end of the country. I knew the worry she was feeling. A few days later the good news came that the tumour had been completely removed and that it was benign (not cancerous). She was sent home less than a week later. I was so happy to get the news that my friend's daughter was okay. I was relieved for everyone.

No parent should have to go through a health scare like that. As I initially walked with my friend through the hard-hitting news (because there was no way of knowing then what was to come), I relived those first days of finding out that Little T, then five months in utero had major heart problems. The deep sadness and fear were suddenly so vivid again. It had mostly been crying at first. I had had a lot of fears for the worst. I had had questions and no sense of when answers would ever come. Looking back now, the tests hadn't provided many answers, they had just generated more questions and the need for more appointments that we then had had to wait anxiously for.

As I watched my dear friend process the waiting, I knew from experience that at some point she couldn't remain in despair, and that she would need to hold on to something and to hope. She shared with me how she was continually praying and relying on God to get her through. Waiting as a parent during an eight-hour surgery must feel like an eternity. She gives God the credit for getting her through that week and the following weeks too, as it takes time to recover from both a successful surgery and the stress of processing the whole experience.

I was surprised when she gave full credit to God for getting her daughter through surgery. It stirred up something very visceral in me. Something that I could probably describe as anger—deep anger. I didn't really think that God had had anything to do with the surgery. That had been the surgeons doing the job that they had been trained for. It was their lifetime dedication to the practice of medicine and not a miracle from on high that had led to a successful outcome. It was the hospital and the country that we live in that had allowed her access to specialized and excellent medical care. You don't have to go far outside of Canada to realize how fortunate we are or how rare this is.

Why would God deserve the credit for the medical care that was given? If He provides it to my friend's daughter and doesn't to a child in Thukuta village, Malawi, does that now make Him less praiseworthy or even not to be trusted? Funny, because Malawi is full of very fervent believers. They are Christians with no access to optometrists or specialized surgeons. The connection to God on these matters can really anger me.

Trust—do I trust God with these matters? I think the answer to that is no. Not anymore. I maybe did before but too much has happened. It has changed my willingness to partake in Christianity as fervently as I once did. It's mainly because I don't want to be around people actively spewing banalities about how "God allows things to happen to us in our life to help our faith in Him grow stronger." Let's break that down and use this same logic with what happened to Little T.

God allowed me to get pregnant after some time had passed, with all the angst and longing to be a mom that goes with that awesome responsibility. After four months of bonding with my child in the womb and emotionally planning and hoping for a bright tomorrow, my husband and I had learned that our baby had serious heart issues. God then allowed my pregnancy to progress for the next four months as we attended countless medical appointments. My body kept changing and growing; with each ultrasound new concerns were mentioned in addition to his serious heart issues. God allowed eight months of life in my womb, only for my child to die without anyone knowing until the next day—at an ultrasound appointment. God then allowed me to give birth to my stillborn child.

I could go on, but I ask—what was God's intention in this? If it was to have my faith grow stronger, I can tell you that it didn't. Over three years later, even though I have a beautiful boy who is happy and healthy at nineteen months of age, my faith is not any stronger, in fact, it has weakened to the point of nearly vanishing.

I don't know why it is still there at all, and why I won't just give up on God entirely.

I knew at sixteen years of age that bad things happen to good people. I read books about it like Where is God When It Hurts? I knew that Job wrestled with God over these issues. Maybe that's why I haven't thrown in the towel so to speak. I still have some wrestling to do.

I don't have anything else to do but to pray for Emma and for Sarah, Blair, Jude, and Elise that God can emotionally support and carry them through this health crisis.

March 12, 2019

Journal Entry

When time slows down, I feel things begin to resurface. It's like the water has calmed down and has become still. This now reveals the rocks along the shore for what they really are—jagged, dangerous edges.

Finn is sleeping through most of the night. When he wakes up, Daniel is the one who responds to him and feeds him. We have settled into a routine where I feel more rested; I am on top of both his and our nutrition. We moved down two floors into our new apartment at the end of October and I have mostly sorted through the remaining boxes. I now have actual time to be still. I have trouble with being still; I am much better at being busy.

I returned to work five months after Little T's passing; the business kept my mind from obsessing about the baby that I wasn't raising. It also gave me something to focus on other than the PTSD symptoms. Months passed. This gave me a year before Daniel and I tried for another baby. I also needed to be busy when I became pregnant again, because those nine months felt like an eternity. I remember websites and apps all saying that the second pregnancy goes by so fast.

That's because you have a little one at home that you are busy caring for. I didn't. What I did have were many reminders of changes in my body, and then sensations that reminded me of the whole relationship that I shared with my first son Little T. And—the physical experience of being pregnant again was awful. It was a worse pregnancy; I had nausea until well over four months, acid reflux, a horrible cold, and a cough that lasted for a month. I wanted it all to be over fast. I wanted to skip to the end and get a chance to finally raise a son.

Things are calm for the moment as I am staying home with Finn for another four months. He is nursing much less and napping at regular times, and I can take more time for myself to care for my physical body. I am exercising, eating better, and sleeping more. I got rid of my maternity and nursing clothes and I can now fit back into older clothes. I feel ready to get some new ones. I feel that in many ways I am finding myself again.

My body is much different now than before both pregnancies.

I suppose I wouldn't want it to go back completely to the way it was before, as I would lose the signs that showed me that Little T was so much a part of me. Getting rid of all the clothes didn't really affect me at the time, but now it pains me to think of that period of my life as being over. There were four years of wearing certain clothes to accommodate pregnancies. I don't want that time again. I am certain of that, but I hate to think of it as just a blip in the life of my wardrobe or just a blip in my life. It wasn't. I didn't think to look through the wardrobe for what connected me most to Little T. I guess they were just clothes.

My body is different now in ways that I would prefer that it wasn't. That was due to two childbirths, but I also can't help but wonder if my first childbirth with Little T affected me more than I know.

It is a time of relative stillness. The winter months will soon come to an end, but the rivers and lakes are still frozen. I find myself mourning. I have time to experience the daily adventures and joys with Finn, but then I can suddenly be stricken with a painful memory, as if I suddenly slipped and winded myself on the ice.

I now have chances to have more moments alone. When I am stricken by a memory or a painful thought, I feel like I don't get back up as fast. That scares me. I don't want to feel like I need to be busy to be well. I love caring for my son and yes, this keeps me busy, but I can't go on looking for things to fill my time just to not be alone with my thoughts.

March 26, 2019

Journal Entry

It was four years ago today that I had been so excited to tell my mom on her birthday that she was going to become a grandmother. I had decided to wrap the positive pregnancy test for her to open. Devon, my brother, realizing what it was, had just said, "Ew gross." Mom had looked at me and had waited for confirmation before she had reacted. She said later that she hadn't wanted to assume the best, as I had told her months earlier to stop pestering Daniel and me about having kids. She, of course, had been ecstatic, as had been the whole family. We had also told Daniel's parents who had been especially excited to get some good news for a change, as both of them had been hospitalized very recently.

It's strange to think of that time again. It had been good news and we had had no idea of what was to come. We simply had had the joy of expecting the baby that we had been hoping for.

April 8, 2019

Journal Entry

I start to feel it when Mother's Day is approaching and it takes one marketing ad to confirm it. I am having bouts of sadness again. It is sadness for a child that I did not get to nurture. I am also feeling sad knowing that I will be back at work in less than three months, so I will not get to be with Finn full time. It makes me want to hold him closer. I am getting myself ready to have more distance and independence from him. It is triggering sadness. It feels like a double dose of it. I am grieving not just the time I won't have with Finn anymore but the time I will never have with Little T.

Spring is having a strange effect on me. Others seem to be cheering up as the snow melts, but I seem to be slipping into melancholy. Instead of being happy to see more people on our daily strolls, it annoys me. I want to be around people and yet now I am having trouble shaking feelings of sadness and despair.

Being at home with Finn during his second year can be quite

lonely. Yet I am very reluctant to meet new people, especially other moms who are also at home. I chat casually with them in play groups, but I don't persist any further. I have been very cautious about letting anyone new into my life ever since we found out that Little T was sick. I don't want to omit his story when talking to people. Yet it is highly personal and not the only thing to know about who I am. I don't feel that it is easy to understand me and what I have been through.

There are people that I knew before we became pregnant with Little T, but who I didn't connect with during that whole time. I have no interest in reconnecting with them now. Too much has happened, and I feel a disconnect as a result. Colleagues, meanwhile, are busy with their own lives and are consumed with work. I also understand that time passes very quickly for them. My effort and commitment are to those who have remained close. Perhaps it is better that the pool of people in our inner circle has gotten smaller because my return to work will inevitably give me less free time outside of family commitments.

The pottery studio seems to be a good avenue to re-explore. Pouring into a creative outlet and connecting with fellow potters, even if superficially, provides me the opportunity to interact with likeminded people, and to be creative and have some fun. The studio, after all, was a huge part of my life very soon after Little T's passing. I have been finishing some pieces I started in 2016. It's interesting to finish them now and to see their start and completion dates.

I recently watched a video about the Japanese art form of repairing broken pottery with gold, silver, or platinum. The symbolism is just beautiful. It is called kintsugi which translates to "golden joinery."

"This unique method celebrates each artifact's unique history by emphasizing its fractures and breaks instead of hiding or disguising them. In fact, kintsugi often makes the repaired piece even more beautiful than the original, revitalizing it with a new look and giving it a second life." [13]

In doing a bit of further research, I realized that there was very little possibility of my being able to learn this technique myself. After all, it is a true art form and a centuries-old tradition; it's not something that one can just pick up on the fly. And yet—I want to carry this same sentiment into some pieces that I am currently making. I picked up a large bowl that I had made in 2016. It was still not fired, and I was able to carve into it what will look like cracks. My hope is to now put a golden coloured glaze in the cracks for firing. The finished product will hopefully look like a kintsugi piece. I share the sentiment with it, that though it is fractured, though broken from grief, it may be more beautiful than it would otherwise have been. It is the physical representation of the healing that I'm attempting within myself.

The Japanese philosophy of wabi-sabi calls for seeing beauty in the flawed or imperfect. What holds true for me is that I do not wish to hide the fractures, my brokenness, or my continued grief. They are still very much a part of me. Perhaps this is the reason that I feel pushed more and more to keep writing. I know that people don't realize how much of a struggle it still is for me. A few months ago I wouldn't have predicted, that when I would be getting ready to go back to work, the loss of Little T would be making that process much harder for me.

Reflections

In May 2019 I decided to find a psychologist to connect with. Finn would soon be starting daycare part time so that he could become used to it before I started work again in July. I felt anxious about this; the thought of being away from him

[13] Kelly Richman-Abdou, Kintsugi: The Centuries-Old Art of Repairing Broken Pottery with Gold (My Modern Met, March 5, 2022). https://mymodernmet.com/kintsugi-kintsukuroi/

when we had been so close for almost two years was almost unbearable. I was also processing my return to work; I wanted to work on my ability to leave time for myself and to not take on too much. I kept myself busy but I was worried that there were thoughts and emotions that I needed to process and not rush past. Sometimes I spoke to Finn about Little T, and I often worried that these conversations were going to have a negative impact on him and might even scar him. I wondered about my parenting and how best to navigate things with Finn moving forward. I also knew that I was continuing to wrestle with my faith, so I found a psychologist who was willing to delve into conversations about spirituality. There was still much to discuss and process, so I began therapy once again.

October 15, 2019

Journal Entry

Annual Perinatal Awareness Day.

The world breaks everyone and afterwards many are strong at the broken places.

—Ernest Hemingway

I experienced a deep trauma . . . and then I felt that I lost my faith. Anger had to be expressed somewhere. I felt that there were suddenly a lot of holes in the cultural belief system that I grew up in. The idea that God led me to this deep trauma, after I had dedicated almost every aspect of my life to serving Him and serving others in love, just didn't fit in my mind's understanding. I didn't stop going to church, but my church closed, and I didn't actively seek another. I already had another home church—my husband's Catholic parish. It was filled with lovely people and was a community centered on social justice. But I didn't feel a push to go, and when I did, I would get emotional during different parts of the service. I didn't want to be seen as that vulnerable in public.

I also knew that I needed a break from my long-established pattern of functioning in a servant role at church. I had given of my time to singing, organizing calendars, making bulletins, sitting on committees, and other activities. I didn't know what it meant to just receive anymore, and I could no longer function in a giving role.

When Little T had first passed, I had not gone to counseling. I had been doing okay, I thought. I had had five months off work, and I had had time to myself to feel my deep sadness. I had had a safe place to do that in, a pottery studio that was just starting up. My time in the studio had usually meant that I would sit at a pottery wheel and have moments where I was essentially pouring tears.

I also had my Mindfulness app. This was a lovely collection of meditations which allowed me to feel my grief but also to take a break from it and to take notice of the other sensory information that existed all around me. I could let the waves of sadness come and go. I could walk in the rain and feel a connection with the water that surrounded me as I cried. I felt God somewhere in the rain as it gently caressed my face. This was the same feeling that I sometimes had when I was swimming or watching waves.

Something with the mindfulness practice really struck me deeply. I knew that I needed it in my life and I knew that it could provide others relief from the pain of deeply difficult emotions. So many of my students at school suffer from anxiety. During my two-year maternity leave, I had come in to the school to give presentations on stress and mindfulness. I now made a big ask and was able to get a room dedicated solely to mindfulness in the school. I was grateful that a budget was available; eager school staff helped me to get the supplies and to do the renovations needed to turn the room into a safe, tranquil, and quiet space. Students could now go there to listen to nature sounds and meditations.

Inspired by the app that brought me so much satisfaction, I

researched some of its narrators and found that one of them followed training in New York City with the Interdependence Project. I went to their website, found a training session that began in September and signed up before I had any real assurance that my professional development money would cover it (I was back at work now). I was committed to attend and eager to have the training. It would allow me to equip students with techniques that would help them better deal with their own suffering.

At the first weekend training session in September I was suddenly hit with the realization that it, and one other session of the six, were going to be focused on developing my own meditative practice. This would mean that I would have to meditate alone for a stretch of time. I would be in silence, sans app, and would have no narrator assistance. This terrified me. Being alone in quiet with my thoughts since Little T's passing had always meant looking back on my trauma, something I actively avoided. Buried thoughts would inevitably surface and sadness would come back. Although these waves were smaller than before, they were waves nonetheless. I had never wanted to lean into this, not since those days in the pottery studio before my grief turned into PTSD. I was very afraid of what would surface.

Our trainer was so delicate and calm. She assured us that difficult things might very well arise, but that we could get relief in those moments by turning to our anchor—our breath or the sounds that we were hearing. This anchor could provide us with a break from the difficulty. Our trainer also provided us with boundaries; we were not there to comfort each other. Should there be a need, she would step in and assist, but our role was to be there. We were to take in the present moment, find our anchor for ourselves, and focus on it.

I gave myself permission to sit in silence. This was for me. I would find my own sensory anchor.

I never liked focusing on my breath. It always felt like it was just something else that I had to control; it was another problem to deal with. Breathing exercises felt like they were just that, exercises. They were something to perform, or evaluate, or get better at, and then to be done with. I preferred listening to sounds, looking at the form of water, or sometimes touching an object like clay. I tried centering with the sounds of 124 East 40th Street, New York City. They were busy sounds and they made me curious as to what was going on around us. I had many thoughts of how this training was going to be good for this student or that student or this friend or . . . my thoughts wouldn't slow down. Then I tried to label them. That thought was compassion, this one was planning. This took up much of my meditation.

The room's air conditioner kicked in. The hum of the machine caused me to think of it as God's presence. I openly thought, "Okay God, you can be here with me at this moment." My thoughts still raced as busy sounds came and went. There were sirens and taxis. A baby cried. I noticed how I didn't cringe. I thought, "Ah—there's a change from not so long ago. That sound would have sent me spiraling in the past." I wanted to be calmer so I consciously thought to myself; "I think I can focus on my breath now." And so I listened to the air, felt my belly rise and fall, noticed the sounds, and felt the air leaving my nostrils.

We switched to a ten-minute silent stretching time. I moved and bent. I lunged and walked. I noticed the fan on the ceiling above and the quiet rhythm it created. We were then back to sitting poses, and I reflected on the sound of the fan. A thought jumped into my mind, "I wonder if that is what it sounds like in the womb?"

Suddenly I was filled with tears as I thought of Little T. The steady quiet rhythm of being in my belly had been all that he had known. I sat with the tears running down my face. I focused on my breath, and took a break from what suddenly felt so deeply heavy. I leaned into the sadness as I felt the loss of what I had never had with him, and how he had never experienced anything of this life except being inside me. My thoughts suddenly changed. I was back with my breath. I took this time to be silent and to be still.

I would explain what happened next as a spiritual awareness, a realization that was passed on to me. It was perhaps even a breakthrough.

Moments before, I had felt deep sadness that Little T knew only the womb. And yet—IT WAS ENOUGH. Being close to me, feeling my breath, and feeling my body vibrations and movements had been enough. It had been enough to feel deeply loved. Even though there had been no words and no physical touch, the closeness, and simply being present, had been enough. I loved Little T unconditionally, even though he had never taken a single breath in this world. Little T didn't get to be introduced to the world outside of my belly, but he did experience this world through me. He had thirty-six weeks to grow—to sway and rock with the gentle motion and rhythms of my body. I would talk and sing to him. Daniel would talk to him too. We would go for walks with Laska together and I want to think that the steady movement in step was something that Little T even looked forward to. We often had music playing and friends over for dancing and even lip synching.

In therapy sessions I would share how I felt guilty that perhaps I had not done enough for Little T. I felt a deep peace now that I had been enough for him, I had been the ocean that he swam in, I had been his world and his universe. I was his mother.

I came back to my anchor and listened to my breath moving in and out. It was back to only me—just me in the moment. I pondered on how Little T had been cared for by me when I was still. Just being still was enough. I am enough. I am enough when I am just still.

I fell quickly into self-criticism and to thoughts that I needed to be doing more, especially more for others. I wondered if I could be as kind to myself and care for myself as much as I had cared for Little T, and still cared for him. What if the love I accepted for myself was one and the same as my love for Little T? He had not needed to do anything but just be. What if I could show myself that same tenderness and understanding?

I noticed again the hum of the air conditioner and its steady presence. I was reminded that the God that I grew up believing in as a child sees me this way all the time. I had forgotten this. In my wrestling with God, I had focused on my feelings towards Him, which consisted mostly of anger. But what about His regard for me? What if my presence was enough? What if I was loved no matter what? What if I didn't have to be always thinking about or planning for others to be significant?

I knew that somewhere deep down my acts of service didn't change anything about the way He saw me. I could just be. I could feel love and be loved at any moment. I could come back to the quiet, still presence again and again. That inner peace was attainable at any moment.

That same day after the training I met up with Daniel in Bryant Park near the New York Public Library. It was a very warm September day. It felt more like a mid-summer day. We sat by the fountain and as the afternoon turned to evening, I shared with him what had happened earlier during the meditation. It felt good to express to him in words all that had been circling in my thoughts in the silent presence of others. His eyes were wide with amazement while I shared how deeply this had all affected me.

Once we returned to Montreal, I would be bringing this all up again in my therapy sessions. I had known that these New York sessions were going to be the time that I really needed to have healing take place. I knew they might allow for a deeper understanding and acceptance of myself. It was the time to begin showing kindness and compassion to myself and the time I could finally begin to realize my limitations. I'm me, that's all there is, and that's enough.

After the training, I went back to another brutal week of hearing about students' sufferings. I felt them deeply. I felt the stress of not getting everything done that was on my desk. My inbox spoke to great needs not yet addressed. And yet, I had gained an ability to be able to come back, again and again—and at any moment—to that stillness and realization that I was enough. I was loved no matter what.

I would explore my faith with my therapist in much greater detail during our sessions that fall. I still needed to embark on some unpacking of what had been blocking me from this inner peace. This was a process that now seemed attainable once again.

> "Behold, I am doing a new thing;
> now it springs forth, do you not perceive it?
> I will make a way in the wilderness
> and rivers in the desert."
> (Isaiah 43:19, English Standard Version)

November 4, 2019

Journal Entry

In my deepest moments of suffering, I had held to a standard. My suffering should be able to teach others something. Since I was a teen, I had felt that others should always be able to look up to me and to learn from me and my experiences. I was deeply convinced that my life should always lead others towards God.

After much therapeutic support I was able to unpack an anger towards my faith and what it had come to represent. My faith was a tool for always serving others. I was deeply angry at the thought that Little T had died simply to teach others a lesson about facing suffering bravely, with God by your side to lean on.

I wanted Little T with me.

When I look back at my blog posts from when Little T was still in my belly, I see things written by a person who had a very naïve outlook. I don't like that part of myself anymore—the hopeful person who was trying to give meaning to every event, activity, or situation. Too much has happened. It has shattered my belief that things can ultimately turn out okay. The firm footing I had at one time is gone. Therapy now helps me to express my inner critic and to look at myself gently just as my therapist does. She expresses compassion for me which helps me to build compassion for myself.

If I want to keep some semblance of my faith it must be packaged differently to make it non-threatening. Using water analogies seems to be permitted. My faith experience has changed. Mindfulness has helped as a way of re-shaping my thinking, my emotions, and my self-talk.

My Christian experience is one that now allows for much more kindness—mainly towards myself. I no longer only exist to serve others. I know that I deserve to live in a state of peace and I don't feel the need to rush from task to task to help everyone at every moment.

Christmas has become and remains an extremely difficult time for me. The preparing for baby Jesus's coming and the songs, reflections, and Scripture passages are all so hard for me.

Last Christmas, while attending the Christmas Eve mass, I had listened to what should have been a beautiful reflection. It had been about Mary's longful expectations for her son. She was contemplating what her dreams for her child had been and how she was letting them go. The wider message had been one of encouraging us all to let go of our expectations for our kids or for others, and to let them become who they needed to become. The message had shattered me inside. There was no more dreaming or longing for what my son would become.

I expect this coming Christmas—and every Christmas moving forward—to have deeply contrasting messages for me. There will be ones of joy, hope, and goodwill—but each will be tied to sadness and grief over what will never be.

July 20, 2020

Journal Entry

Little T was our first child. That's the one you worry about and fret over every second. Even though we didn't get to watch him grow up and take his first steps, we did worry, and we watched every ultrasound with wonder, excitement, and fear. He taught us a lot about what we couldn't control in the world. That we would wish to prevent something bad from happening to him was an inevitable outcome, right from the first time that we saw his arms moving and his heart beating.

We knew that we couldn't stay paralyzed in fear. We instead chose joy throughout the pregnancy. We continued to wonder at him and to stay in the present moment without looking too far into the uncertain future.

After Little T had passed away and I became pregnant with Finn, I openly voiced all my fears to my psychiatrist. I wondered what kind of a mother I could possibly be; I feared that my sadness would rub off on Finn. Daniel and I wanted our child to live a full and joyful life and to not be limited by the possibility of something bad happening.

The oldest child gets to pave the way for his younger siblings, and Little T managed to do that for his younger brother. Daniel and I again chose joy, even though we still lacked control and we could have chosen to live in fear. No one would have blamed us for it.

My psychiatrist reassured me that it wasn't whether I would have moments of sadness or not that would make me a good mother. Instead, the important thing was that I would give my emotions space to just be, and that I wouldn't shut them out or close them off somewhere. During my grief I had also learned how to take care of myself and to give allowance to the fact that I was worth caring for. She assured me that this would do wonders to get through parenthood.

She was right.

In my recent therapy sessions with my psychologist, she has helped me to realize that not only does Finn get a parent who takes the time when she needs it to recharge and come back patient again, but he also hears from us that he is allowed to feel and express his own emotions and can take the time to feel them so that they don't control him. While Daniel and I were exhausted going through parenthood with Finn, we were fortunate enough to have previously worked through many of the communication issues between us. As well, I had developed a deeper sense of awareness of when my patience had run out and when I was in need of replenishing.

October 15, 2020

Journal Entry

Pregnancy and Infant Loss Awareness Day.

We are between fall leaves and winter snow.

Grief is cyclical, just like the seasons. As November approaches, I hold my breath and expect sadness to resurface. I know every year it is coming, but October's beautiful fall colours help me to forget. Halloween's whimsical pageantry lets me embark on an adventure and pumpkin pie and apple crisp take over my senses for a while.

Just when the leaves had almost all fallen, my mourning

began. I immediately felt like I had nothing to hope for and once again I was sure that the sadness would surely take me over.

Despite the touch of frost, I continued my walks. Over the last weeks I had been observing the trees attentively. Their leaves had slowly changed and eventually had started to fall. The days passed and I continued watching as they performed their final autumn bow. Now the trees were bare; all that was left were their stark, still figures.

Stillness is not something that I welcome. Fearful that painful memories will overtake me, I have developed a pattern of keeping busy and avoiding too much solitude. Walks are one thing that help me to tolerate the still moments as my attention can be captivated by my ever alert senses.

I was fearful of a long November. It's the first month after summer with short days and long dark evenings. The skies are grey and the ground barren. What is there to see in between fall leaves and the winter snow?

Consequential dates came. I had to endure them as memories flooded in. Rainy days were a chance to let out tears under the privacy of an umbrella while I moved along an empty path.

Between thoughts, I spotted the striking colours of the tree trunks as water trickled down them. The soaked leaves glimmered on the ground. With no more leaves on the branches, I noticed the view to the river was now clear. Water was rushing by. The memories weren't as heavy to walk with. Like the river's flow, the weighty thoughts came but they were quickly swept away.

I will welcome a new season now. It will be dark and dreary, but beautiful. In between the fall leaves and the winter snow, I will leave room to remember whom I never want to forget.

May 9, 2021

Journal Entry

Little T—Honouring Mother's Day instead of celebrating it.

The first Mother's Day after losing Little T may have marked the onset of my PTSD.

It wasn't even going through the day itself that hurt, but the anticipation of it. Hearing ads on TV or radio, or any marketing email for Mother's Day gifts would send me into a spiral of sadness, anger, and a feeling like someone had punched me in the gut.

I didn't get to live the joy of being a mother to Little T. Instead, I had an empty womb and baby blankets and gifts that were tucked away in boxes. Not because my child had grown up but because I would never get to see him grow up.

Every Mother's Day since has still been difficult. My family knows to not bring it up and my mother knows that I will approach her if I feel up to doing something. It pains me to take the celebration away from her as she has always been a loving and caring mother and grandmother and she deserves to be celebrated.

Daniel said to me that I deserved to hear this—if not on that day but at some point—that Finn was a lucky boy to have me as his mother.

I wonder if I could rephrase the day. Instead of celebrating Mother's Day, what if I could honour it? I would honour what I did not get a chance to have with Little T. I would honour that I still love him and always will. I would honour the dedication my mother had and still has. I would honour what my mother-in-law gives to me, to Daniel, and to Finn. I would honour myself for the mother that I am to Finn.

As Mother's Day approaches, I will continue to unpack more. I will be honouring the memories and honouring the old and new feelings that surface as motherhood seems to bring with it a wide range of emotions. Thanks to therapy, I have finally allowed anger to be present. I learnt to be at peace with it, accept it, and allow it. This is something I think we struggle with as women. It is something that society disapproves of and reproaches us for, and it is something we even discourage each other from feeling and expressing.

Since I have been able to be more at peace with my anger, I have been kinder with my mom, and I am letting her in more. I also don't judge myself so much for being harsh with my mom in the past.

My mother is an amazing grandmother. Love for Finn flows out of her, and their relationship is a beautiful thing to witness. My mother has her own story to tell, and I am sure that she is processing her own griefs. My mother is a beautiful example of resiliency.

The baby blanket and stuffed plush T-Rex have now become Finn's. But he knows that they first belonged to his brother. Finn is four now. Just recently he started to bring up his brother and to ask questions. He asks why he died, he says that he misses him, and he thinks that he will eventually meet him. I even showed Finn Little T's baby box of pictures, bracelet, and clothes. It made me very sad but also happy that we were remembering Little T together on Mother's Day. Even though Finn doesn't quite understand, he is taking away from this the fact that Little T is loved, that he matters, and that we are taking the time to remember him.

September 20, 2021

Holding the sadness of life in our heart while never forgetting the beauty of the world and the goodness of being alive.

—Trungpa Rinpoche

Journal Entry

I went for a walk by the water this morning with our dog, Laska. Daniel and Finn had already left for work and daycare, and I took advantage of a day where I could work from home and get a slower start. My thoughts were already racing about the day, so I tried to switch my attention to Laska and then the river. I noticed the burrs by the path and remembered that yesterday Finn had rolled down the same hill and had got some on him. It made me smile. Then I thought to myself that remembering him and this memory of him felt both scary and familiar at the same time. A panic crept in. What if he also passes away like Little T and I have nothing left but memories?

I took a breath and looked again at the river. I let myself identify with what was going on—fear and sadness. But then there was also joy. I was back on the path, next to the water walking Laska. I took another step and then another. I noticed the leaves. They were starting to change colours now. I thought to myself that I better enjoy every moment of their colourful display.

I eventually turned onto the path to return home, feeling better than when I had begun.

Reflections

I see in my work how parenting and anxiety can have an impact on a child. I think that without support I would have been a different parent. I would have tried to protect Finn at all costs and to remove dangers wherever I saw them. Because of what had happened with Little T, I would have been justified in constantly feeling fear and acting on it. I still have this fear, but I am better equipped now to ask the question each time: Do I want Finn to thrive or to survive? I have to move past the moment of fear. With the lockdown ending, had I not been equipped to handle anxiety, and had I not built an understanding of gradual exposure to a feared danger, I might not have embraced Finn being in school, playing with peers, and being part of activities, trips, and adventures like I do now.

Ever since my time in New York with the Interdependence Project, I have continued to closely carry the gift of mindful awareness. This means that at any moment I can stop to gain perspective. I can kindly allow what I am feeling and give it space, but I can also anchor myself by tapping into my senses or my breath so that I don't feel swept away by the intensity.

Without having been introduced to mindfulness, I would not have slowed down and found a better pace. I would not have allowed for all my emotions to be present so that I could see them more clearly, accept them with gentleness, and eventually move past them. I keep very busy, but it would have become unsustainable, and the anxiety would have taken me over. The narrative I told myself would also have continued to be one of criticism rather than the one of self-acceptance that I try to maintain now.

I explain mindfulness to students to help them disengage from overwhelming thoughts and emotions or to bring down the intensity of what they are feeling. It's as if they are lowering the volume dial of their intense feelings and tuning in to a quieter and softer sound.

October 15, 2021

Journal Entry

Pregnancy and Infant Loss Awareness Day.

When I think of grief and the trauma that I've experienced, I still can't say that it has been fully resolved. There is never a solution or total end to grief. I have never agreed with the term "finding resolution in your loss." I will always hate and disagree with this term. I will never accept that "everything happens for a reason" or that "this was meant to happen." Those words will never come out of my mouth when I am talking to someone else who is experiencing a loss.

As I spoke to my son this evening before bed, I told him that I would never stop loving him. Never ever. I feel the same thing for Little T as I feel for him. What has changed as time has passed and as I have given myself the space and permission to feel, is that the sadness: "Isn't associated with a feeling of heaviness or a quality of pulling me back." (Dalai Lama, as quoted by Pema Chödrön). It is just an integrated part of me now.

November 2, 2021

Journal Entry

Yesterday Daniel and I both took the day off and Finn stayed home from daycare. We took time as a family last year as well. We didn't make any big plans but let Finn direct what we were going to do with our day. I was determined to set up his room to incorporate his growing toy collection. I have imparted to Finn a love of dinosaurs and the movie Jurassic Park. The original is still too scary, but some time ago we did watch the Netflix cartoon Camp Cretaceous. This has led to him having a growing dinosaur collection. He says that his favorite dinosaur is a T-Rex. At the secondhand store we picked up another dinosaur toy magnet board with dinosaur pictures and fossils.

The evening was more difficult once Finn was in bed. I remembered the night of November 1 and where I had been when I felt a strange sensation in my stomach. It hadn't been painful but had been different than anything I had experienced during the pregnancy. The next day had been the ultrasound where we learned of Little T's passing.

Today I took the day off. I spent time reading my blog posts and journaling. I took out the shoebox of Little T's keepsakes from the hospital. I cried for a long while; it felt like I hadn't done so in a long time. Though it was painful, honouring him by taking the day gave me peace.

I took time in the pottery studio on my own and took out the pieces I had carefully glued back together. These were some of my favorite pieces. Now when I am in the studio I listen to the church service at our community Catholic church. Without needing to be physically present I can listen in and feel a part of these shared rituals. I don't feel anger anymore. Instead, I welcome the reflection time and the familiar songs. Passages are read out loud and I think of one that I hold onto now: "And the peace of God that surpasses all understanding will guard your hearts and minds in Christ Jesus." Philippians 4:7 (New English Translation)

I went out to get myself a coffee and soil for my plants, as I had some that were multiplying and that would soon need to be placed in new pots. I had never gardened before Finn and Little T. It had seemed like a futile hobby. In the March before Finn turned two, we had started growing plants from seeds. My first summer was not very successful. I grew only pepper plants, and none really took off. In March 2020, the day before the COVID lockdown began, I once again started the vegetable seeds. It gave me something to watch and focus on. As the months flowed on and the isolation became tiresome, I continued to watch and nurture our plants. (I have noticed that since I began planting, the springs aren't as tough anymore, and that the cyclical nature of things has helped me.)

Returning from the plant store I observed the trees on our street. Now, waiting for the last leaves to fall, I look for the beauty in November.

My evening was spent listening to Daniel and Finn play and joining them for a last dinosaur attack. We read books about kindness and about taking breaths when you are caught up in difficult emotions. I lay in his room and waited until he drifted off to sleep.

I gave space today. Space to remember as I don't want to forget.

Reflections

Looking back on the summer of 2022.

Daniel, Finn, and I went to British Columbia this summer to visit Jeff, Sasha, Audrey, and Jack. It was so much fun to be with them all again and to see how much Audrey and Jack had grown in two and a half years. We stayed in North Vancouver and visited the family on their houseboat on the water. We walked by the waterway every day and went on excursions on the dinghy and watched seals. We went to the aquarium and various markets and took ferry boats almost daily. Finn and Audrey played in the water park by the shipyards. It was so nice to be that close to the ocean.

Finn and I stayed on in British Columbia for an extra week and we took a train ride to see Sarah and Blair, and their kids Emma, Jude, and Elise in Kamloops. Elise, who was born in December 2015, was now six and a half. We spent five days at their house and the kids played while Sarah and I talked and had many heart-to-heart conversations. Sarah asked me if it was hard to see Elise. I had already reflected on this and told her that no, it surprised me, but no, not really. Elise is a confident and goofy girl and a lot of fun to be with.

It helps to remember how old Little T would have been when I see how old Elise is. I'm not wrought with sadness to watch her grow. I had felt robbed that I didn't get to see Elise grow up along with the other two, Jude and Emma. I did not seem them much for a whole year. I needed distance at the time. Then they moved. Now I felt some gratitude that even though we were robbed of time, it hadn't seemed to have mattered at all. Finn was playing with the three kids and together they all had a blast. Sarah and I talked and laughed as if no time had really passed.

I think back to when I had found out about Emma's brain tumour and the emotions I had gone through regarding faith. I realize now that without psychological help and mindfulness over the last two years, I would never have unpacked my spiritual upbringing in order to understand that I was always set on serving others and forgetting that I, too, mattered and was loved. Otherwise, I may have thrown away my faith altogether and lost all ability for hope. Sarah's friendship has always been one where I can be open and honest about my wrestling with faith, Sarah's friendship and others like it have kept me connected to my faith.

I reflect back on my therapy sessions. If not for the support that I had received, I would still be having trouble setting limits and saying no at work. I would not have taken time for my own passions, and I I would still be holding on to an assumption that taking time for myself was unnecessary and not a priority, compared to caring for others both at work and as a parent to Finn. This led me to reflect on the space work was taking in my life and to begin making space for a renewed passion in art. In March I applied to return to university part time to pursue studies in fine arts--specifically in art education. I was accepted and started back in the fall, part time. I continued to work four days a week at the high school.

September 12, 2022

Journal Entry

Meg is currently going through in vitro treatments. She received a late diagnosis of endometriosis, which is a disease in which tissue, like the lining of the uterus, grows outside the uterus. She has therefore struggled with the prospects of having a very low chance of bearing a child.

Today was an amazing day. Passing her wildest expectations, she had a healthy embryo transferred into her uterus. We now wait to hear if the implantation successfully happened, and if a baby is growing. We ate supper together: my sister, her husband, my parents, Daniel, Finn, and me. There was a lot of hope and delight. My parents couldn't contain themselves. I found myself surprised at how their reactions affected me. My parents are planning for their grandchild. It was all too familiar, and it brought back a lot of pain.

I am not so sure how I will navigate this moving forward. On the one hand, it doesn't bother me to be hopeful for my sister. I am excited and now frequently pray for the little one who is hopefully taking shape inside of her. On the other hand, how do I separate how my parents feel and express their emotions from how I take this in, or rather, how I take this on? It's this empathy that I exaggerate in my mind to protect others from heartache. I want to protect my parents from going through the pain of losing a grandchild once again. I don't want them to go through months of hope only for it to be shattered.

I suppose they are stronger and more resilient than I think. Perhaps I should look with gratitude on the fact that they can still express delight and uncontrollable joy for my sister, and can celebrate with her a moment that she never thought possible.

Maybe I am more resilient than I give myself credit for. I continue to feel deeply, especially tonight. I continue to mourn and grieve the life that we never had with Little T. This is particularly true when I experience triggering moments and am reminded of the pain it caused those I love. Yet, I can still speak with my sister about allowing there to be hope. If her worst fear happens, she can feel it then. She will be surrounded by people who she can lean on. I don't look back and regret the hope that we had with Little T.

The times I tried to protect myself from what I felt or when I tried to shelter others from their own emotions is when I was suffering the most. That is when the distance grew and I felt the most alone.

I am angry still that Little T did not survive. That eight months of hope left my family shattered and without a child to welcome. I am angry that for years I was a different person than before. I was less hopeful and unable to express in person what I was going through. I was also embittered, and more easily irritable and impatient towards others' seemingly small sufferings compared to mine.

My more joyful and sociable self has resurfaced in the last couple of years. I don't think there was any other way to go through the grief and post-traumatic stress except via all the difficult emotions that I felt and the changes that happened within me. I am grateful to those who remained patient, or rather to those who just let me be exactly who I was in those moments. Writing has been my very best outlet to express with truth what I was feeling. Writing blog posts was a way at certain points to let others know what I was feeling, at a safer distance than in person, and it helped people to understand me better and to give me space.

When I wrote posts, I wanted people to know that I was okay. As time passed, I needed to post less. I wanted as well to write a journal just for me, without all the filtering and excusing. It wasn't going to be a product to be used for someone else's benefit. I came to the computer to type, feel, breathe, and release. There were times when I needed it more, and then months and months would go by without me feeling the urge or need to write at all.

As time went on, journaling became something that I also wanted to do to help remember Little T. I often wrote on the anniversary of his passing. Often on those days I would re-read my writing and then journal again with new insights that I had gathered over that year. As I write now, I flow through thoughts more easily than in the past. I don't think this means I care any less about little T. I don't question my heart. I know that he is always present there.

Even tonight I feel less tightness in my chest than when I took in my parents' excitement. Once I was alone, tears were shed instead of stopped. Emotions were named instead of ignored. I can acknowledge that this is not over. Grief continues to crash over me as a wave onto the shore. But it doesn't pull me under like a riptide. Instead, I watch the ripples forming and breaking and the rocks being pushed around and then released. They are smoother and more reflective now. They have been submerged in the water, shaped by the force of the waves, and contoured, rounded, and formed by the irresistible energy of the surf.

September 27, 2022

Journal Entry

My sister had a miscarriage. I am leaving her and her husband space to be, to feel, to process, and to grieve.

My first reaction on hearing the news was to problem solve and to try to find solutions for them. That's how I react to others' sufferings—I go into active-duty mode. It took some time, but now I am coming around to sadness.

I did not like feeling helpless and that there might not be a solution to this. I wanted so much for her to not feel pain; I wanted her to be spared of what I went through. But I can't shelter her from this and my experience has taught me that there really isn't anything to say. I am grateful that they have each other to lean on.

I look back and am thankful that Daniel and I had each other and that he allowed me to experience grief in whatever form it took. I needed time to express the anger I felt. When I finally did, it made me an angrier person to be around. This was unusual for our dynamic where we both valued calm and respectful communication, while still finding space to express feelings and frustrations in the relationship. I sensed that Daniel was uncomfortable with my anger. At one point, though, he insisted that he didn't want me to filter myself; he knew that he just needed to find a way to deal with it. His process was different than mine. He reads as a pastime, but literature is also a passion of his. It is maybe not surprising then that he was processing things through what he read.

When I was allowing myself to initially express my anger, Daniel was reading a lot of women writers, some who delved into the topic of anger. It shaped his understanding of me and affected how he would later react. While he never intentionally made me feel that my anger was too much to handle, it is the takeaway that I had. I think it may be embedded in girls, at least of my and previous generations, that emotions that don't serve others should be channeled into something positive.

But there is nothing positive in the loss of a child or of a potential child. The emotions and words that we have at our disposal barely scratch at the inner turmoil. I am happy that Daniel is willing to adapt and give space to me so that I can express and feel anger as it comes up. It made us stronger as it helped me to feel that I had the space to express what I was going through without being judged.

October, 2022

Journal Entry

My paintings have been connected to themes of grief partly because of the time of year that I have often done my painting. I have been writing again and reflecting on some of my previous writings; I then return to painting class and continue to express what I am sorting through. Writing and then painting. Painting and then writing. This has been leading me to further self-discovery. I was thinking in one of my recent painting classes about how painting—physically moving colour around on the canvas—had helped what were otherwise intense emotions to flow and move about outside of my head. In that way I had been able to observe them better and possibly make sense of them.

What might be the most powerful therapy, though, is that I

have been able to speak about my grief with others through the presenting of my paintings in class.

January 23, 2023

I am about to put away the Christmas tree decorations and two of them are memorials of Little T. One is a star with the footprints of Little T on it. Another is an ultrasound picture. Even if it brings on some sadness, I want to remember Little T and to feel that he shares in the Christmas season with us. Tonight before bed, Finn shows me how the little stuffed T-Rex dinosaur is the one that he is choosing to have in bed with him that night.

He says, "His name is Little T, Momma," and then, "Why did Little T die in your tummy, Momma?"

I reply, "Little T had holes in his heart and the doctors could not go into my tummy to repair them. They were waiting for him to come out so that they could repair them, but his heart stopped before he could come out."

He asks, "Were you sad, Momma?"

"Yes."

"You wanted to have a boy, and then you had me." He hugs me.

"I love you both, I love Little T still and I love you.

"You will see Little T someday, after you die, in heaven."

"Yes, I will."

"And when I die, I will see him, too."

As quickly as he has brought up the subject, he changes it; we start to read the book he has chosen by his favorite author, Robert Munsch. Bedtime and reading together is always filled with joy and laughter. No matter how hard the day is or if bedtime has been a huge ordeal to get going, we always end the night with reading together. Daniel and I take turns reading to Finn.

I lie with Finn until he has fallen asleep listening to his bedtime playlist. Among the Beatles songs, "All You Need Is Love" plays.

January 27, 2023

Journal entry

My sister is pregnant! Her journey with infertility, in vitro, miscarriage, have been difficult. Her resilience and commitment are beautiful. Now, because of how far I have come, I am there to watch as both a close observer and as her sister as she goes through the pain and the fearful journey of a high-risk pregnancy. I am available emotionally to accompany her, and I have learned in my experience to be a good listener, and to watch out for what she needs from me.

I can also speak openly about my experiences with her now, and she seems to want to hear about them, especially now that she is in the early stages of her pregnancy with its many uncertainties. She is holding on to hope and, after getting through many layers of my own grief, I am at a place where I, too, can hold on to hope once again. I know we are a source of strength for each other. I know I will need to lean on my coping strategies as I relive moments of my own pregnancies by witnessing hers. Prayers keep flowing out of me for her and the child that she is growing.

(In September 2023, she gave birth to a beautiful and healthy girl).

March 2023

A *Writing from Daniel*

Speech Writing Conference Exercise.

I just remember standing still.
It's stupid in a way. We weren't actually standing there.
But everyone else was walking or bustling in the subway station.
Turnstiles churned people to and from work, schools, and homes.
And yet, there we were.
We had just received the news that our son was one in a million.
You've probably heard parents say that hundreds of times.
Ours was too, though not how we hoped.
An ultrasound showed that he had a rare heart condition, and we had just left the hospital.
Now, standing on a platform in the middle of a busy Wednesday afternoon, Liz and I were sinking.
And we didn't know if we could get out.
We were told that our Little T—short for Little T-Rex—had to grow as much as possible in the womb.
We were told that he had to make it to thirty-six weeks in the pregnancy for him to have a chance.
We had a goal.
So, things started to normalize.
At first, we went to the hospital once every few weeks.
Then, once a week.
Then, twice a week.
Every time, it was the same thing. Squirt gel on Liz's belly, assess Little T's progress, and repeat.
Gel, assess, repeat.
Gel, assess, repeat.
Our therapist said that the process helped the doctors to feel that they were in control.
But they weren't.
We made it to thirty-six weeks. In fact, we made it to

thirty-six weeks and three days.
That day, we went to the hospital. Liz lifted her shirt to show her belly. It had grown significantly since that day in the subway station.
Gel, assess.
Little T's wild heart had stopped racing.
We had fallen through the subway station platform.
The stories of our children are ones that never have an end.
That includes the ones that are so unfairly taken from us.
We try to keep Little T's legacy alive.
He brought us so much joy in a time of great darkness. He left a mark even though he never took a breath of air.
Today, our second son, Finnegan, is five years old.
He's healthy, happy, and altogether wild in the best possible way.
He also knows about Little T.
He sleeps with a stuffed T-Rex that we had originally bought for our Little T-Rex.
And when we look at them together, we're no longer stuck on that subway station platform.
Little T and Finnegan reached down to pull us out.

July 1st, 2024

Journal entry

As another school year closes, I have been reflecting on my role at the school. Making more room for my renewed passion in art over the past two years has enabled a spark in me to grow.

I know that writing, painting, reflecting and my work in therapy have led me to understand myself better & started to quiet the need to always serve others above myself.

Taking care of other people's mental health needs has taken its toll on me. I realize that I am tired and need to focus on filling my cup first. As a result, I am resigning from my role and will continue school full time to become an art teacher.

In my twenties when I first started University, I was in art education but switched to youth and childhood intervention. At that time, I knew that I would be consumed with the students in my class who were suffering and singularly focusing on getting them the support they needed. I have enjoyed the 15 years of keeping that focus. Now I want to focus on my passion for art and transmitting that to others.

July 4th, 2024

Journal entry

Today is Finn's 7th birthday. He insisted Daniel and I take the day off, and so we went to the zoo and water park together. Once there, we found our way to the wave pool. Finn is an adventurer and, like in most activities, he did not hold back as he swam further in the water. A lifeguard eventually told him to stay behind the line because of his age, yet he took great joy crashing against the waves.

As I watched him, I felt fear and dread surface in me. What if the waves were too much? What if one of them overwhelmed him? Then I stopped myself and observed his reactions. He was having a blast.

I reminded myself that despite our tragic experience with Little T, Daniel and I are raising Finn to live life to the fullest. We want his experiences to be full of joy and void of fear.

He is thriving both in the water and out of it.

Back at the waterpark, I changed my perspective and watched the waves. I started to ride them alongside him. I was delighted by his reactions, and he laughed and smiled at mine. As a wave broke and splashed us, he turned to me and said, "That was a good one!"

EPILOGUE

Reflection, Introspection, and Taking Stock of Motherhood

I am thankful to you, dear reader, for taking the time to learn about my experiences. I hope my journey helped you understand what someone who has lived through perinatal loss may be dealing with internally. I hope it has provided you with a window into the grief experience—whatever the personal loss.

I am at a much different place than when I first began to write my blog. I like to think that I have grown as a person, and that I am more self-assured. I hope that I am a little less judgmental of my own thoughts, emotions, and experiences; more honest with myself; and able to find the time and space to feel things and find avenues to express them.

Since I was a teenager, I have found it difficult to prioritize my own mental health because I have a tendency to care for those around me first. I have seen my students suffer from performance anxiety and depression, and how negative self-talk and unreasonable objectives only make matters worse.

As women, we rarely take the time to check in with ourselves when we try to get pregnant, experience pregnancy and raise our children. We also seldom seek out support when we need it. Our protective maternal instincts can also take over and make us feel guilty when we haven't protected our children from all danger. We need more platforms to talk and support one another. Navigating these waters is difficult and often lonely.

I hope my book will encourage women to reach out when they need support, prioritize time for themselves and find outlets for self-expression.

There is a beauty in the emotional partnership that we share as women, friends, mothers, sisters, and daughters. That union binds and helps sustain us, so long as gentle, loving care and vulnerability are present.

I am more aware now than ever of the universal suffering women face when dealing with pregnancy loss or difficulty trying to conceive. Yet, I am frustrated that these issues are seldom spoken about. My mom's adopted mother experienced many losses in pregnancy, and she never got support. When she couldn't conceive after eight miscarriages, she turned to adoption. Soon after, she gave birth to a daughter of her own, and my mom suffered through a childhood of feeling unwanted and unwelcome. She was hurt by a woman who had been hurting herself.

How did my mother not only survive but thrive? She spent much of her childhood in nature, found her faith, and she empathized with her mother's experience. She eventually started a career as a social worker and family counsellor to help others get through emotional turmoil.

My sister has also dealt with in vitro fertilization, miscarriage and pregnancy complications. Her experience stems from her endometriosis diagnosis, a disease that is little talked about and severly underfunded. Increasingly, I learn of friends, colleagues, and many other women who have gone through miscarriages or perinatal loss, and I wonder why I heard so little before.

I feel a need to speak loudly, to scream aloud, that we matter, that we suffer, that we are strong, and that we are resilient. We must empower the women in our lives to thrive, not just to survive. We deserve care, time, and support. We should not have to put on a brave face to get past these heartbreaking experiences. We are neither untouched nor unscathed. Instead, we must acknowledge that our losses affect us deeply, both emotionally and physically, and can change us forever.

My wish is that my story is one of hope—of waves bravely tackled. Rather than having the heartbreak of perinatal loss create lasting, irreparable damage, I worked hard to overcome what seemed utterly insurmountable at the time.

I am very grateful for the support I have in my life. I have a caring and supportive family, and so does my husband. Even if I felt alone at times, I never was. The days in the hospital and giving birth to Little T would have been unbearable without the presence of our families. I can't imagine what they would have been like alone.

Little T has marked my life forever. He has stitched into the fabric of my very being an understanding of loss and of love that I can never express in full. He provided a window into others' experiences.

I loved this Bible passage when I was younger. In fact, I wrote it in the front of my own copy:

"... the Father of compassion and the God of all comfort, who comforts us in all our troubles, so that we can comfort those in any trouble with the comfort we ourselves have received from God. 2"

Corinthians 1:3-4 (Berean Standard Bible)

I hated this passage for several years.

Now, I am at a place where those words share the same meaning for me as they did years ago, only in my present moment. I have embraced a new understanding and can offer it to others. Completing this book and sharing my story is an acknowledgement that I embrace this passage to the core. That's not to say that I would celebrate the pain and ask for it again. But I know that through my sharing, Little T keeps having an impact on this world. This means everything to me as a mother.

www.ingramcontent.com/pod-product-compliance
Lightning Source LLC
Chambersburg PA
CBHW040903120626
46551CB00006B/618